A. Strahan

A journey to the western islands of Scotland

A. Strahan

A journey to the western islands of Scotland

ISBN/EAN: 9783743347441

Manufactured in Europe, USA, Canada, Australia, Japa

Cover: Foto ©Andreas Hilbeck / pixelio.de

Manufactured and distributed by brebook publishing software (www.brebook.com)

A. Strahan

A Journey to the western islands of Scotland

A JOURNEY

TO THE

WESTERN ISLANDS

OF

SCOTLAND.

A NEW EDITION.

LONDON:

Printed for A. STRAHAN; and T. CADELL, in the Strand.

MDCCXCI.

Strand, Oct. 26, 1785.

☞ SINCE this Work was printed off, the Publisher having been informed that the Author, some years ago, had promised the Laird of Rasay, to correct, in a future edition, a passage concerning him, p. 133, thinks it a justice due to that Gentleman to insert here the Advertisement relative to this matter, which was published, by Dr. Johnson's desire, in the Edinburgh Newspapers in the year 1775, and which has been lately reprinted in Mr. Boswell's *Tour to the Hebrides:*

" *The Authour of the* Journey *to the Western Islands, having related that the* Macleods *of* Rasay *acknowledge the chieftainship, or superiority, of the* Macleods *of* Sky, *finds that he has been misinformed or mistaken. He means in a future edition to correct his errour, and wishes to be told of more, if more have been discovered.*"

A

JOURNEY

TO THE

WESTERN ISLANDS

OF

SCOTLAND.

I HAD defired to vifit the *Hebrides*, or Weftern Iflands of Scotland, fo long, that I fcarcely remember how the wifh was originally excited; and was, in the Autumn of the year 1773, induced to undertake the journey, by finding in Mr. Bofwell a companion, whofe acutenefs would help my inquiry, and whofe gaiety of converfation and civility of manners are fufficient to counteract

counteract the inconveniencies of travel, in countries less hospitable than we have passed.

On the eighteenth of August we left Edinburgh, a city too well known to admit description, and directed our course northward, along the eastern coast of Scotland, accompanied the first day by another gentleman, who could stay with us only long enough to shew us how much we lost at separation.

As we crossed the *Frith* of *Forth*, our curiosity was attracted by *Inch Keith*, a small island, which neither of my companions had ever visited, though, lying within their view, it had all their lives solicited their notice. Here, by climbing with some difficulty over shattered crags, we made the first experiment of unfrequented coasts. Inch Keith is nothing more than a rock covered with a thin
layer

layer of earth, nor wholly bare of grafs, and very fertile of thiftles. A fmall herd of cows grazes annually upon it in the fummer. It feems never to have afforded to man or beaft a permanent habitation.

We found only the ruins of a fmall fort, not fo injured by time but that it might be eafily reftored to its former ftate. It feems never to have been intended as a place of ftrength, nor was built to endure a fiege, but merely to afford cover to a few foldiers, who perhaps had the charge of a battery, or were ftationed to give fignals of approaching danger. There is therefore no provifion of water within the walls, though the fpring is fo near, that it might have been eafily enclofed. One of the ftones had this infcription: " Maria Reg. " 1564." It has probably been neglected from the time that the whole ifland had the fame king.

We left this little island with our thoughts employed awhile on the different appearance that it would have made, if it had been placed at the same distance from London, with the same facility of approach; with what emulation of price a few rocky acres would have been purchased, and with what expensive industry they would have been cultivated and adorned.

When we landed, we found our chaise ready, and passed through *Kinghorn*, *Kirkaldy*, and *Cowpar*, places not unlike the small or straggling market-towns in those parts of England where commerce and manufactures have not yet produced opulence.

Though we were yet in the most populous part of Scotland, and at so small a distance from the capital, we met few passengers.

The

The roads are neither rough nor dirty; and it affords a fouthern ftranger a new kind of pleafure to travel fo commodioufly without the interruption of toll-gates. Where the bottom is rocky, as it feems commonly to be in Scotland, a fmooth way is made indeed with great labour, but it never wants repairs; and in thofe parts where adventitious materials are neceffary, the ground once confolidated is rarely broken; for the inland commerce is not great, nor are heavy commodities often tranfported otherwife than by water. The carriages in common ufe are fmall carts, drawn each by one little horfe; and a man feems to derive fome degree of dignity and importance from the reputation of poffeffing a two-horfe cart.

ST. ANDREWS.

At an hour fomewhat late we came to St. Andrews, a city once archiepifcopal;

where that university still subsists in which philosophy was formerly taught by Buchanan, whose name has as fair a claim to immortality as can be conferred by modern latinity, and perhaps a fairer than the instability of vernacular languages admits.

We found, that by the interposition of some invisible friend, lodgings had been provided for us at the house of one of the professors, whose easy civility quickly made us forget that we were strangers; and in the whole time of our stay we were gratified by every mode of kindness, and entertained with all the elegance of lettered hospitality.

In the morning we rose to perambulate a city, which only history shews to have once flourished, and surveyed the ruins of ancient magnificence, of which even the ruins cannot long be visible, unless some care be taken to preserve them; and where

is

is the pleasure of preserving such mournful memorials? They have been till very lately so much neglected, that every man carried away the stones who fancied that he wanted them.

The cathedral, of which the foundations may be still traced, and a small part of the wall is standing, appears to have been a spacious and majestick building, not unsuitable to the primacy of the kingdom. Of the architecture, the poor remains can hardly exhibit, even to an artist, a sufficient specimen. It was demolished, as is well known, in the tumult and violence of Knox's reformation.

Not far from the cathedral, on the margin of the water, stands a fragment of the castle, in which the archbishop anciently resided. It was never very large, and was built with more attention to security than pleasure. Cardinal Beatoun is said to have had workmen employed in improving its fortifications at the time when he was murdered by the ruffians of reformation, in the manner of which Knox has given what he himself calls a merry narrative.

The change of religion in Scotland, eager and vehement as it was, raifed an epidemical enthufiafm, compounded of fullen fcrupuloufnefs and warlike ferocity, which, in a people whom idlenefs refigned to their own thoughts, and who converfing only with each other, fuffered no dilution of their zeal from the gradual influx of new opinions, was long tranfmitted in its full ftrength from the old to the young, but by trade and intercourfe with England, is now vifibly abating, and giving way too faft to that laxity of practice and indifference of opinion, in which men, not fufficiently inftructed to find the middle point, too eafily fhelter themfelves from rigour and conftraint.

The

The city of St. Andrews, when it had loſt its archiepiſcopal pre-eminence, gradually decayed: One of its ſtreets is now loſt; and in thoſe that remain there is the ſilence and ſolitude of inactive indigence and gloomy depopulation.

The univerſity, within a few years, conſiſted of three colleges, but is now reduced to two; the college of St. Leonard being lately diſſolved by the ſale of its buildings and the appropriation of its revenues to the profeſſors of the two others. The chapel of the alienated college is yet ſtanding, a fabrick not inelegant of external ſtructure; but I was always, by ſome civil excuſe, hindered from entering it. A decent attempt, as I was ſince told, has been made to convert it into a kind of green-houſe, by planting its area with ſhrubs. This new method of gardening is unſucceſsful; the plants do not hitherto proſper. To what uſe it will next be put, I have no pleaſure

pleasure in conjecturing. It is something, that its present state is at least not ostentatiously displayed. Where there is yet shame, there may in time be virtue.

The dissolution of St. Leonard's College was doubtless necessary; but of that necessity there is reason to complain. It is surely not without just reproach, that a nation, of which the commerce is hourly extending, and the wealth increasing, denies any participation of its prosperity to its literary societies; and while its merchants or its nobles are raising palaces, suffers its universities to moulder into dust.

Of the two colleges yet standing, one is by the institution of its founder appropriated to Divinity. It is said to be capable of containing fifty students; but more than one must occupy a chamber. The library, which is of late erection, is not very spacious, but elegant and luminous.

The

The doctor, by whom it was shewn, hoped to irritate or subdue my English vanity, by telling me, that we had no such repository of books in England.

St. Andrews seems to be a place eminently adapted to study and education, being situated in a populous, yet a cheap country, and exposing the minds and manners of young men neither to the levity and dissoluteness of a capital city, nor to the gross luxury of a town of commerce, places naturally unpropitious to learning; in one the desire of knowledge easily gives way to the love of pleasure, and in the other, is in danger of yielding to the love of money.

The students however are represented as at this time not exceeding a hundred. Perhaps it may be some obstruction to their increase that there is no episcopal chapel in the place. I saw no reason reafon for imputing their paucity to the prefent profeffors; nor can the expence of an academical education be very reafonably objected. A ftudent of the higheft clafs may keep his annual feffion, or as the Englifh call it, his term, which lafts feven months, for about fifteen pounds, and one of lower rank for lefs than ten; in which, board, lodging, and inftruction are all included.

The chief magiftrate refident in the univerfity, anfwering to our vice-chancellor, and to the *rector magnificus* on the continent, had commonly the title of Lord Rector; but being addreffed only as *Mr. Rector* in an inauguratory fpeech by the prefent chancellor, he has fallen from his former dignity of ftyle. Lordfhip was very liberally annexed by our anceftors to any ftation or character of dignity: They faid, the *Lord General,* and *Lord Ambaffador;* fo we ftill fay, *my Lord,* to the judge upon the circuit,

circuit, and yet retain in our Liturgy *the Lords of the Council.*

In walking among the ruins of religious buildings, we came to two vaults over which had formerly stood the house of the sub-prior. One of the vaults was inhabited by an old woman, who claimed the right of abode there, as the widow of a man whose ancestors had possessed the same gloomy mansion for no less than four generations. The right, however it began, was considered as established by legal prescription, and the old woman lives undisturbed. She thinks however that she has a claim to something more than sufferance; for as her husband's name was Bruce, she is allied to royalty, and told Mr. Boswell that when there were persons of quality in the place, she was distinguished by some notice; that indeed she is now neglected, but she spins a thread, has the company of her cat, and is troublesome to nobody.

Having now seen whatever this ancient city offered to our curiosity, we left it with good wishes, having reason to be highly pleased with the attention that was paid us. But whoever surveys the world must see many things that give him pain. The kindness of the professors did not contribute to abate the uneasy remembrance of an university declining, a college alienated, and a church profaned and hastening to the ground.

St. Andrews indeed has formerly suffered more atrocious ravages and more extensive destruction, but recent evils affect with greater force. We were reconciled to the sight of archiepiscopal ruins. The distance of a calamity from the present time seems to preclude the mind from contact or sympathy. Events long paſt are barely known; they are not conſidered. We read with as little emotion the violence of Knox and his followers, as the irruptions of Alaric and the Goths. Had the univerſity been deſtroyed two centuries ago, we ſhould not have regretted it; but to ſee it pining in decay and ſtruggling for life, fills the mind with mournful images and ineffectual wiſhes.

ABERBROTHICK.

As we knew ſorrow and wiſhes to be vain, it was now our buſineſs to mind our way. The roads of Scotland afford little diverſion to the traveller, who ſeldom ſees himſelf either encountered or overtaken, and who has nothing to contemplate but grounds that have no viſible boundaries, or are ſeparated by walls of looſe ſtone. From the bank of the Tweed to St. Andrews

drews I had never seen a single tree, which I did not believe to have grown up far within the present century. Now and then about a gentleman's house stands a small plantation, which in Scotch is called a *policy*, but of these there are few, and those few all very young. The variety of sun and shade is here utterly unknown. There is no tree for either shelter or timber. The oak and the thorn is equally a stranger, and the whole country is extended in uniform nakedness, except that in the road between *Kirkaldy* and *Cowpar*, I passed for a few yards between two hedges. A tree might be a show in Scotland as a horse in Venice. At St. Andrews Mr. Boswell found only one, and recommended it to my notice; I told him that it was rough and low, or looked as if I thought so. This, said he, is nothing to another a few miles off. I was still less delighted to hear that another tree was not to be seen nearer. Nay, said a gentleman

gentleman that stood by, I know but of this and that tree in the county.

The Lowlands of Scotland had once undoubtedly an equal portion of woods with other countries, Forests are every where gradually diminished, as architecture and cultivation prevail by the increase of people and the introduction of arts. But I believe few regions have been denuded like this, where many centuries must have passed in waste without the least thought of future supply. Davies observes in his account of Ireland, that no Irishman had ever planted an orchard. For that negligence some excuse might be drawn from an unsettled state of life, and the instability of property; but in Scotland possession has long been secure, and inheritance regular, yet it may be doubted whether before the Union any man between Edinburgh and England had ever set a tree.

Of this improvidence no other account can be given than that it probably began in times of tumult, and continued becaufe it had begun. Eftablifhed cuftom is not eafily broken, till fome great event fhakes the whole fyftem of things, and life feems to recommence upon new principles. That before the Union the Scots had little trade and little money, is no valid apology; for plantation is the leaft expenfive of all methods of improvement. To drop a feed into the ground can coft nothing, and the trouble is not great of protecting the young plant, till it is out of danger; though it muft be allowed to have fome difficulty in places like thefe, where they have neither wood for palifades, nor thorns for hedges.

Our way was over the Firth of Tay, where, though the water was not wide, we paid four fhillings for ferrying the chaife. In Scotland the neceffaries of life are eafily procured,

procured, but superfluities and elegancies are of the same price at least as in England, and therefore may be considered as much dearer.

We stopped a while at Dundee, where I remember nothing remarkable, and mounting our chaise again, came about the close of the day to Aberbrothick.

The monastery of Aberbrothick is of great renown in the history of Scotland. Its ruins afford ample testimony of its ancient magnificence: Its extent might, I suppose, easily be found by following the walls among the grass and weeds, and its height is known by some parts yet standing. The arch of one of the gates is entire, and of another only so far dilapidated as to diversify the appearance. A square apartment of great loftiness is yet standing; its use I could not conjecture, as its elevation was very disproportionate to its area. Two corner towers particularly attracted our attention. Mr. Bofwell, whofe inquifitivenefs is feconded by great activity, fcrambled in at a high window, but found the ftairs within broken, and could not reach the top. Of the other tower we were told that the inhabitants fometimes climbed it, but we did not immediately difcern the entrance, and as the night was gathering upon us, thought proper to defift. Men fkilled in architecture might do what we did not attempt: They might probably form an exact groundplot of this venerable edifice. They may from fome parts yet ftanding conjecture its general form, and perhaps by comparing it with other buildings of the fame kind and the fame age, attain an idea very near to truth. I fhould fcarcely have regretted my journey, had it afforded nothing more than the fight of Aberbrothick.

MON-

MONTROSE.

Leaving these fragments of magnificence, we travelled on to Montrose, which we surveyed in the morning, and found it well built, airy, and clean. The town-house is a handsome fabrick with a portico. We then went to view the English chapel, and found a small church, clean to a degree unknown in any other part of Scotland, with commodious galleries, and what was yet less expected, with an organ.

At our inn we did not find a reception such as we thought proportionate to the commercial opulence of the place; but Mr. Boswell desired me to observe that the innkeeper was an Englishman, and I then defended him as well as I could.

When I had proceeded thus far, I had opportunities of observing what I had never heard, that there were many beggars in Scotland. In Edinburgh the proportion is, I think, not lefs than in London, and in the fmaller places it is far greater than in Englifh towns of the fame extent. It muft, however, be allowed that they are not importunate, nor clamorous. They folicit filently, or very modeftly, and therefore though their behaviour may ftrike with more force the heart of a ftranger, they are certainly in danger of miffing the attention of their countrymen. Novelty has always fome power, an unaccuftomed mode of begging excites an unaccuftomed degree of pity. But the force of novelty is by its own nature foon at an end; the efficacy of outcry and perfeverance is permanent and certain.

The road from Montrofe exhibited a continuation of the fame appearances. The country is ftill naked, the hedges are of ftone, and the fields fo generally plowed
that

that it is hard to imagine where grafs is found for the horfes that till them. The harveft, which was almoft ripe, appeared very plentiful.

Early in the afternoon Mr. Bofwell obferved that we were at no great diftance from the houfe of Lord Monboddo. The magnetifm of his converfation eafily drew us out of our way, and the entertainment which we received would have been a fufficient recompence for a much greater deviation.

The roads beyond Edinburgh, as they are lefs frequented, muft be expected to grow gradually rougher; but they were hitherto by no means incommodious. We travelled on with the gentle pace of a Scotch driver, who having no rivals in expedition, neither gives himfelf nor his horfes unneceffary trouble. We did not affect the impatience we did not feel, but were satisfied with the company of each other as well riding in the chaise, as sitting at an inn. The night and the day are equally solitary and equally safe; for where there are so few travellers, why should there be robbers?

ABERDEEN.

We came somewhat late to Aberdeen, and found the inn so full, that we had some difficulty in obtaining admission, till Mr. Boswell made himself known: His name overpowered all objection, and we found a very good house and civil treatment.

I received the next day a very kind letter from Sir Alexander Gordon, whom I had formerly known in London, and after a cessation of all intercourse for near twenty years met here professor of physic in the King's College. Such unexpected renewals

renewals of acquaintance may be numbered among the moſt pleaſing incidents of life.

The knowledge of one profeſſor ſoon procured me the notice of the reſt, and I did not want any token of regard, being conducted wherever there was any thing which I defired to ſee, and entertained at once with the novelty of the place, and the kindneſs of communication.

To write of the cities of our own iſland with the ſolemnity of geographical deſcription, as if we had been caſt upon a newly diſcovered coaſt, has the appearance of very frivolous oſtentation; yet as Scotland is little known to the greater part of thoſe who may read theſe obſervations, it is not ſuperfluous to relate, that under the name of Aberdeen are compriſed two towns ſtanding about a mile diſtant from each other,

other, but governed, I think, by the same magiftrates.

Old Aberdeen is the ancient epifcopal city, in which are ftill to be feen the remains of the cathedral. It has the appearance of a town in decay, having been fituated in times when commerce was yet unftudied, with very little attention to the commodities of the harbour.

New Aberdeen has all the buftle of profperous trade, and all the fhow of increafing opulence. It is built by the waterfide. The houfes are large and lofty, and the ftreets fpacious and clean. They build almoft wholly with the granite ufed in the new pavement of the ftreets of London, which is well known not to want hardnefs, yet they fhape it eafily. It is beautiful and muft be very lafting.

What particular parts of commerce are chiefly exercifed by the merchants of Aberdeen, I have not inquired. The manufacture which forces itfelf upon a ftranger's eye is that of knit-ftockings, on which the women of the lower clafs are vifibly employed.

In each of thefe towns there is a college, or in ftricter language, an univerfity; for in both there are profeffors of the fame parts of learning, and the colleges hold their feffions and confer degrees feparately, with total independence of one on the other.

In Old Aberdeen ftands the King's College, of which the firft prefident was *Hector Boece*, or *Boethius*, who may be juftly reverenced one of the revivers of elegant learning. When he ftudied at Paris, he was acquainted with *Erafmus*, who afterwards gave him a publick teftimony of

his

his esteem, by inscribing to him a catalogue of his works. The style of Boethius, though, perhaps, not always rigorously pure, is formed with great diligence upon ancient models, and wholly uninfected with monastic barbarity. His history is written with elegance and vigour, but his fabulousness and credulity are justly blamed. His fabulousness, if he was the author of the fictions, is a fault for which no apology can be made; but his credulity may be excused in an age, when all men were credulous. Learning was then rising on the world; but ages so long accustomed to darkness, were too much dazzled with its light to see any thing distinctly. The first race of scholars in the fifteenth century, and some time after, were, for the most part, learning to speak, rather than to think, and were therefore more studious of elegance than of truth. The contemporaries of Boethius thought it sufficient to know what the ancients had delivered.

The

The examination of tenets and of facts was reserved for another generation.

Boethius, as president of the university, enjoyed a revenue of forty Scottish marks, about two pounds four shillings and sixpence of sterling money. In the present age of trade and taxes, it is difficult even for the imagination so to raise the value of money, or so to diminish the demands of life, as to suppose four and forty shillings a year, an honourable stipend; yet it was probably equal, not only to the needs, but to the rank of Boethius. The wealth of England was undoubtedly to that of Scotland more than five to one, and it is known that Henry the Eighth, among whose faults avarice was never reckoned, granted to Roger Ascham, as a reward of his learning, a pension of 10 pounds a year.

The other, called the Marischal College, is in the new town. The hall is large and well lighted.

lighted. One of its ornaments is the picture of Arthur Johnston, who was principal of the college, and who holds among the Latin poets of Scotland the next place to the elegant Buchanan.

In the library I was shewn some curiosities; a Hebrew manuscript of exquisite penmanship, and a Latin translation of Aristotle's Politicks by *Leonardus Aretinus*, written in the Roman character with nicety and beauty, which, as the art of printing has made them no longer necessary, are not now to be found. This was one of the latest performances of the transcribers, for Aretinus died but about twenty years before typography was invented. This version has been printed, and may be found in libraries, but is little read; for the same books have been since translated both by *Victorius* and *Lambinus*, who lived in an age more cultivated; but perhaps owed in

part

part to *Aretinus* that they were able to excel him. Much is due to those who first broke the way to knowledge, and left only to their successors the task of smoothing it.

In both these colleges the methods of instruction are nearly the same; the lectures differing only by the accidental difference of diligence, or ability in the professors. The students wear scarlet gowns and the professors black, which is, I believe, the academical dress in all the *Scottish* universities, except that of Edinburgh, where the scholars are not distinguished by any particular habit. In the King's College there is kept a publick table, but the scholars of the Marischal College are boarded in the town. The expence of living is here, according to the information that I could obtain, somewhat more than at St. Andrews.

The courſe of education is extended to four years, at the end of which thoſe who take a degree, who are not many, become maſters of arts, and whoever is a maſter may, if he pleaſes, immediately commence doctor. The title of doctor, however, was for a conſiderable time beſtowed only on phyſicians. The advocates are examined and approved by their own body; the miniſters were not ambitious of titles, or were afraid of being cenſured for ambition; and the doctorate in every faculty was commonly given or ſold into other countries. The miniſters are now reconciled to diſtinction, and as it muſt always happen that ſome will excel others, have thought graduation a proper teſtimony of uncommon abilities or acquiſitions.

The indiſcriminate collation of degrees has juſtly taken away that reſpect which they originally claimed as ſtamps, by which the literary value of men ſo diſtinguiſhed

was

was authoritatively denoted. That academical honours, or any others, should be conferred with exact proportion to merit, is more than human judgment or human integrity have given reason to expect. Perhaps degrees in univerſities cannot be better adjuſted by any general rule, than by the length of time paſſed in the public profeſſion of learning. An Engliſh or Iriſh doctorate cannot be obtained by a very young man, and it is reaſonable to ſuppoſe, what is likewiſe by experience commonly found true, that he who is by age qualified to be a doctor, has in ſo much time gained learning ſufficient not to diſgrace the title, or wit ſufficient not to deſire it.

The Scotch univerſities hold but one term or ſeſſion in the year. That of St. Andrews continues eight months, that of Aberdeen only five, from the firſt of November to the firſt of April.

In Aberdeen there is an English chapel, in which the congregation was numerous and splendid. The form of public worship used by the church of England is in Scotland legally practised in licensed chapels, served by clergymen of English or Irish ordination, and by tacit connivance quietly permitted in separate congregations supplied with ministers by the successors of the bishops who were deprived at the Revolution.

We came to Aberdeen on Saturday August 21. On Monday we were invited into the town-hall, where I had the freedom of the city given me by the Lord Provost. The honour conferred had all the decorations that politeness could add, and what I am afraid I should not have had to say of any city south of the Tweed, I found no petty officer bowing for a fee.

The

The parchment containing the record of admiffion, is with the feal appending, faftened to a riband, and worn for one day by the new citizen in his hat.

By a lady who faw us at the chapel, the Earl of Errol was informed of our arrival, and we had the honour of an invitation to his feat, called Slanes Caftle, as I am told, improperly, from the caftle of that name, which once ftood at a place not far diftant.

The road beyond Aberdeen grew more ftony, and continued equally naked of all vegetable decoration. We travelled over a tract of ground near the fea, which, not long ago, fuffered a very uncommon and unexpected calamity. The fand of the fhore was raifed by a tempeft in fuch quantities, and carried to fuch a diftance, that an eftate was overwhelmed and loft. Such and fo hopelefs was the barrennefs fuperinduced, that the owner, when he was required to pay the usual tax, desired rather to resign the ground.

SLANES CASTLE. THE BULLER OF BUCHAN.

We came in the afternoon to *Slanes Castle*, built upon the margin of the sea, so that the walls of one of the towers seem only a continuation of a perpendicular rock, the foot of which is beaten by the waves. To walk round the house seemed impracticable. From the windows the eye wanders over the sea that separates Scotland from Norway, and when the winds beat with violence, must enjoy all the terrifick grandeur of the tempestuous ocean. I would not for my amusement wish for a storm; but as storms, whether wished or not, will sometimes happen, I may say without violation of humanity, that I should willingly look out upon them from Slanes Castle.

When

When we were about to take our leave, our departure was prohibited by the Countefs, till we fhould have feen two places upon the coaft, which fhe rightly confidered as worthy of curiofity, *Dun Buy*, and the *Buller of Buchan*, to which Mr. Boyd very kindly conducted us.

Dun Buy, which in Erfe is faid to fignify the *Yellow-Rock*, is a double protuberance of ftone, open to the main fea on one fide, and parted from the land by a very narrow channel on the other. It has its name and its colour from the dung of innumerable fea-fowls, which in the Spring chufe this place as convenient for incubation, and have their eggs and their young taken in great abundance. One of the birds that frequent this rock has, as we were told, its body not larger than a duck's, and yet lays eggs as large as thofe of a goofe. This bird is by the inhabitants

bitants named a *Coot*. That which is called *Coot* in England, is here a *Cooter*.

Upon these rocks there was nothing that could long detain attention, and we soon turned our eyes to the *Buller*, or *Bouilloir* of *Buchan*, which no man can see with indifference, who has either sense of danger or delight in rarity. It is a rock perpendicularly tubulated, united on one side with a high shore, and on the other rising steep to a great height, above the main sea. The top is open, from which may be seen a dark gulf of water which flows into the cavity, through a breach made in the lower part of the inclosing rock. It has the appearance of a vast well bordered with a wall. The edge of the Buller is not wide, and to those that walk round, appears very narrow. He that ventures to look downward sees, that if his foot should slip, he must fall from his dreadful elevation

vation upon stones on one side or into the water on the other. We however went round, and were glad when the circuit was completed.

When we came down to the sea, we saw some boats, and rowers, and resolved to explore the Buller, at the Bottom. We entered the arch, which the water had made, and found ourselves in a place, which, though we could not think ourselves in danger, we could scarcely survey without some recoil of the mind. The bason in which we floated was nearly circular, perhaps thirty yards in diameter. We were inclosed by a natural wall, rising steep on every side to a height which produced the idea of insurmountable confinement. The interception of all lateral light caused a dismal gloom. Round us was a perpendicular rock, above us the distant sky, and below an unknown profundity of water. If I had any malice against a walking spirit, instead of laying him in the Red-sea, I would condemn him to reside in the Buller of Buchan.

But terrour without danger is only one of the sports of fancy, a voluntary agitation of the mind that is permitted no longer than it pleases. We were soon at leisure to examine the place with minute inspection, and found many cavities which, as the watermen told us, went backward to a depth which they had never explored. Their extent we had not time to try; they are said to serve different purposes. Ladies come hither sometimes in the summer with collations, and smugglers make them storehouses for clandestine merchandise. It is hardly to be doubted but the pirates of ancient times often used them as magazines of arms, or repositories of plunder.

To the little vessels used by the northern rowers, the Buller may have served as a
shelter

shelter from storms, and perhaps as a retreat from enemies; the entrance might have been stopped, or guarded with little difficulty, and though the vessels that were stationed within would have been battered with stones showered on them from above, yet the crews would have lain safe in the caverns.

Next morning we continued our journey, pleased with our reception at Slanes Castle, of which we had now leisure to recount the grandeur and the elegance; for our way afforded us few topics of conversation. The ground was neither uncultivated nor unfruitful; but it was still all arable. Of flocks or herds there was no appearance. I had now travelled two hundred miles in Scotland, and seen only one tree not younger than myself.

BAMFF.

BAMFF.

We dined this day at the houfe of Mr. Frazer of *Streichton*, who fhewed us in his grounds fome ftones yet ftanding of a druidical circle, and what I began to think more worthy of notice, fome foreft trees of full growth.

At night we came to Bamff, where I remember nothing that particularly claimed my attention. The ancient towns of Scotland have generally an appearance unufual to Englifhmen. The houfes, whether great or fmall, are for the moft part built of ftones. Their ends are now and then next the ftreets, and the entrance into them is very often by a flight of fteps, which reaches up to the fecond ftory. The floor which is level with the ground, being entered only by ftairs defcending within the houfe.

The

The art of joining squares of glass with lead is little used in Scotland, and in some places is totally forgotten. The frames of their windows are all of wood. They are more frugal of their glass than the English, and will often, in houses not otherwise mean, compose a square of two pieces, not joining like cracked glass, but with one edge laid perhaps half an inch over the other. Their windows do not move upon hinges, but are pushed up and drawn down in grooves, yet they are seldom accommodated with weights and pullies. He that would have his window open must hold it with his hand, unless what may be sometimes found among good contrivers, there be a nail which he may stick into a hole, to keep it from falling.

What cannot be done without some uncommon trouble or particular expedient, will not often be done at all. The incommodiousness of the Scotch windows keeps them

them very closely shut. The necessity of ventilating human habitations has not yet been found by our northern neighbours; and even in houses well built and elegantly furnished, a stranger may be sometimes forgiven, if he allows himself to wish for fresher air.

These diminutive observations seem to take away something from the dignity of writing, and therefore are never communicated but with hesitation, and a little fear of abasement and contempt. But it must be remembered, that life consists not of a series of illustrious actions, or elegant enjoyments; the greater part of our time passes in compliance with necessities, in the performance of daily duties, in the removal of small inconveniencies, in the procurement of petty pleasures; and we are well or ill at ease, as the main stream of life glides on smoothly, or is ruffled by small obstacles and frequent interruption.

The

The true ſtate of every nation is the ſtate of common life. The manners of a people are not to be found in the ſchools of learning, or the palaces of greatneſs, where the national character is obſcured or obliterated by travel or inſtruction, by philoſophy or vanity; nor is public happineſs to be eſtimated by the aſſemblies of the gay, or the banquets of the rich. The great maſs of nations is neither rich nor gay: they whoſe aggregate conſtitutes the people, are found in the ſtreets, and the villages, in the ſhops and farms; and from them collectively conſidered, muſt the meaſure of general proſperity be taken. As they approach to delicacy a nation is refined, as their conveniencies are multiplied, a nation, at leaſt a commercial nation, muſt be denominated wealthy.

ELGIN.

ELGIN.

Finding nothing to detain us at Bamff, we set out in the morning, and having breakfasted at Cullen, about noon came to *Elgin*, where in the inn, that we supposed the best, a dinner was set before us, which we could not eat. This was the first time, and except one, the last, that I found any reason to complain of a Scottish table; and such disappointments, I suppose, must be expected in every country, where there is no great frequency of travellers.

The ruins of the cathedral of Elgin afforded us another proof of the waste of reformation. There is enough yet remaining to shew, that it was once magnificent. Its whole plot is easily traced. On the north side of the choir, the chapter-house, which is roofed with an arch of stone, remains entire; and on the south side, another mass of building, which we could

could not enter, is preserved by the care of the family of Gordon; but the body of the church is a mass of fragments.

A paper was here put into our hands, which deduced from sufficient authorities the history of this venerable ruin. The church of Elgin had, in the intestine tumults of the barbarous ages, been laid waste by the irruption of a highland chief, whom the bishop had offended; but it was gradually restored to the state, of which the traces may be now discerned, and was at last not destroyed by the tumultuous violence of Knox, but more shamefully suffered to dilapidate by deliberate robbery and frigid indifference. There is still extant, in the books of the council, an order, of which I cannot remember the date, but which was doubtless issued after the reformation, directing that the lead, which covers the two cathedrals of Elgin and Aberdeen, shall be taken away,

away, and converted into money for the support of the army. A Scotch army was in those times very cheaply kept; yet the lead of two churches must have born so small a proportion to any military expence, that it is hard not to believe the reason alleged to be merely popular, and the money intended for some private purse. The order however was obeyed; the two churches were stripped, and the lead was shipped to be sold in Holland. I hope every reader will rejoice that this cargo of sacrilege was lost at sea.

Let us not however make too much haste to despise our neighbours. Our own cathedrals are mouldering by unregarded dilapidation. It seems to be part of the despicable philosophy of the time to despise monuments of sacred magnificence, and we are in danger of doing that deliberately, which the Scots did not do but in the unsettled state of an imperfect constitution.

Those

Those who had once uncovered the cathedrals never wished to cover them again: and being thus made useless, they were first neglected, and perhaps, as the stone was wanted, afterwards demolished.

Elgin seems a place of little trade, and thinly inhabited. The episcopal cities of Scotland, I believe, generally fell with their churches, though some of them have since recovered by a situation convenient for commerce. Thus *Glasgow*, though it has no longer an archbishop, has risen beyond its original state by the opulence of its traders; and *Aberdeen*, though its ancient stock had decayed, flourishes by a new shoot in another place.

In the chief street of Elgin, the houses jut over the lowest story, like the old buildings of timber in London, but with greater prominence; so that there is sometimes a walk for a considerable length under a cloister, or portico, which is now indeed frequently broken, because the new houses have another form, but seems to have been uniformly continued in the old city.

FORES. CALDER. FORT GEORGE.

We went forwards the same day to Fores, the town to which Macbeth was travelling, when he met the weird sisters in his way. This to an Englishman is classic ground. Our imaginations were heated, and our thoughts recalled to their old amusements.

We had now a prelude to the Highlands. We began to leave fertility and culture behind us, and saw for a great length of road nothing but heath; yet at *Fochabars*, a seat belonging to the duke of Gordon, there is an orchard, which in

Scotland

Scotland I had never seen before, with some timber trees, and a plantation of oaks.

At Fores we found good accommodation, but nothing worthy of particular remark, and next morning entered upon the road, on which *Macbeth* heard the fatal prediction; but we travelled on not interrupted by promises of kingdoms, and came to *Nairn*, a royal burgh, which, if once it flourished, is now in a state of miserable decay; but I know not whether its chief annual magistrate has not still the title of Lord Provost.

At Nairn we may fix the verge of the Highlands; for here I first saw peat fires, and first heard the *Erse* language. We had no motive to stay longer than to breakfast, and went forward to the house of Mr. *Macaulay*, the minister who published an account of *St. Kilda*, and by his direction visited Calder Castle, from which

Macbeth drew his second title. It has been formerly a place of strength. The draw-bridge is still to be seen, but the moat is now dry. The tower is very ancient. Its walls are of great thickness, arched on the top with stone, and surrounded with battlements. The rest of the house is later, though far from modern.

We were favoured by a gentleman, who lives in the castle, with a letter to one of the officers at Fort George, which being the most regular fortification in the island, well deserves the notice of a traveller, who has never travelled before. We went thither next day, found a very kind reception, were led round the works by a gentleman, who explained the use of every part, and entertained by Sir *Eyre Coote*, the governor, with such elegance of conversation as left us no attention to the delicacies of his table.

Of

Of Fort George I shall not attempt to give any account. I cannot delineate it scientifically, and a loose and popular description is of use only when the imagination is to be amused. There was everywhere an appearance of the utmost neatness and regularity. But my suffrage is of little value, because this and Fort *Augustus* are the only garrisons that I ever saw.

We did not regret the time spent at the fort, though in consequence of our delay we came somewhat late to *Inverness*, the town which may properly be called the capital of the Highlands. Hither the inhabitants of the inland parts come to be supplied with what they cannot make for themselves: Hither the young nymphs of the mountains and valleys are sent for education, and as far as my observation has reached, are not sent in vain.

INVERNESS.

Inverness was the last place which had a regular communication by high roads with the southern counties. All the ways beyond it have, I believe, been made by the soldiers in this century. At *Inverness* therefore *Cromwell*, when he subdued *Scotland*, stationed a garrison, as at the boundary of the Highlands. The soldiers seem to have incorporated afterwards with the inhabitants, and to have peopled the place with an English race; for the language of this town has been long considered as peculiarly elegant.

Here is a castle, called the castle of Macbeth, the walls of which are yet standing. It was no very capacious edifice, but stands upon a rock so high and steep, that I think it was once not accessible, but by the help of ladders, or a bridge. Over against

against it, on another hill, was a fort built by *Cromwell*, now totally demolished; for no faction of Scotland loved the name of *Cromwell*, or had any desire to continue his memory.

Yet what the Romans did to other nations, was in a great degree done by Cromwell to the Scots; he civilized them by conquest, and introduced by useful violence the arts of peace. I was told at *Aberdeen* that the people learned from Cromwell's soldiers to make shoes and to plant kail.

How they lived without kail, it is not easy to guess: They cultivate hardly any other plant for common tables, and when they had not kail they probably had nothing. The numbers that go barefoot are still sufficient to shew that shoes may be spared; they are not yet considered as necessaries of life; for tall boys, not otherwife meanly dreſſed, run without them in the ſtreets and in the iſlands; the ſons of gentlemen paſs ſeveral of their firſt years with naked feet.

I know not whether it be not peculiar to the Scots to have attained the liberal, without the manual arts, to have excelled in ornamental knowledge, and to have wanted not only the elegancies, but the conveniencies of common life. Literature, ſoon after its revival, found its way to *Scotland*, and from the middle of the ſixteenth century, almoſt to the middle of the ſeventeenth, the politer ſtudies were very diligently purſued. The Latin poetry of *Deliciæ Poëtarum Scotorum* would have done honour to any nation, at leaſt till the publication of *May's Supplement* the Engliſh had very little to oppoſe.

Yet men thus ingenious and inquiſitive were content to live in total ignorance of the

the trades by which human wants are supplied, and to supply them by the grossest means. Till the Union made them acquainted with English manners, the culture of their lands was unskilful, and their domestick life unformed; their tables were coarse as the feasts of Eskimeaux, and their houses filthy as the cottages of Hottentots.

Since they have known that their condition was capable of improvement, their progress in useful knowledge has been rapid and uniform. What remains to be done they will quickly do, and then wonder, like me, why that which was so necessary and so easy was so long delayed. But they must be for ever content to owe to the English that elegance and culture, which, if they had been vigilant and active, perhaps the English might have owed to them.

Here

Here the appearance of life began to alter. I had seen a few women with plaids at *Aberdeen*; but at *Inverness* the Highland manners are common. There is I think a kirk, in which only the Erse language is used. There is likewise an English chapel, but meanly built, where on Sunday we saw a very decent congregation.

We were now to bid farewell to the luxury of travelling, and to enter a country upon which perhaps no wheel has ever rolled. We could indeed have used our post-chaise one day longer, along the military road to Fort *Augustus*, but we could have hired no horses beyond Inverness, and we were not so sparing of ourselves, as to lead them, merely that we might have one day longer the indulgence of a carriage.

At Inverness therefore we procured three horses for ourselves and a servant, and one more

more for our baggage, which was no very heavy load. We found in the courfe of our journey the convenience of having difencumbered ourfelves, by laying afide whatever we could fpare; for it is not to be imagined without experience, how in climbing crags, and treading bogs, and winding through narrow and obftructed paffages, a little bulk will hinder, and a little weight will burden; or how often a man that has pleafed himfelf at home with his own refolution, will, in the hour of darknefs and fatigue, be content to leave behind him every thing but himfelf.

LOUGH NESS.

We took two Highlanders to run befide us, partly to fhew us the way, and partly to take back from the fea-fide the horfes, of which they were the owners. One of them was a man of great livelinefs and activity, of whom his companion faid,

that

that he would tire any horse in Inverness. Both of them were civil and ready-handed. Civility seems part of the national character of Highlanders. Every chieftain is a monarch, and politeness, the natural product of royal government, is diffused from the laird through the whole clan. But they are not commonly dextrous: their narrowness of life confines them to a few operations, and they are accustomed to endure little wants more than to remove them.

We mounted our steeds on the thirteenth of August, and directed our guides to conduct us to Fort Augustus. It is built at the head of Lough Ness, of which *Inverness* stands at the outlet. The way between them has been cut by the soldiers, and the greater part of it runs along a rock, levelled with great labour and exactness, near the water-side.

Most

Most of this day's journey was very pleasant. The day, though bright, was not hot; and the appearance of the country, if I had not seen the Peak, would have been wholly new. We went upon a surface so hard and level, that we had little care to hold the bridle, and were therefore at full leisure for contemplation. On the left were high and steep rocks shaded with birch, the hardy native of the North, and covered with fern or heath. On the right the limpid waters of *Lough Ness* were beating their bank, and waving their surface by a gentle agitation. Beyond them were rocks sometimes covered with verdure, and sometimes towering in horrid nakedness. Now and then we espied a little corn-field, which served to impress more strongly the general barrenness.

Lough Ness is about twenty-four miles long, and from one mile to two miles broad. It is remarkable that *Boethius*, in his description

scription of Scotland, gives it twelve miles of breadth. When historians or geographers exhibit false accounts of places far distant, they may be forgiven, because they can tell but what they are told; and that their accounts exceed the truth may be justly supposed, because most men exaggerate to others, if not to themselves: but *Boethius* lived at no great distance; if he never saw the lake, he must have been very incurious, and if he had seen it, his veracity yielded to very slight temptations.

Lough Ness, though not twelve miles broad, is a very remarkable diffusion of water without islands. It fills a large hollow between two ridges of high rocks, being supplied partly by the torrents which fall into it on either side, and partly, as is supposed, by springs at the bottom. Its water it remarkably clear and pleasant, and is imagined by the natives to be medicinal. We were told, that it is in some places a
hundred

hundred and forty fathom deep, a profundity scarcely credible, and which probably those that relate it have never founded. Its fish are salmon, trout, and pike.

It was said at Fort *Augustus*, that *Lough Ness* is open in the hardest winters, though a lake not far from it is covered with ice. In discussing these exceptions from the course of nature, the first question is, whether the fact be justly stated. That which is strange is delightful, and a pleasing error is not willingly detected. Accuracy of narration is not very common, and there are few so rigidly philosophical, as not to represent as perpetual, what is only frequent, or as constant, what is really casual. If it be true that *Lough Ness* never freezes, it is either sheltered by its high banks from the cold blasts, and exposed only to those winds which have more power to agitate than congeal; or it is kept in perpetual motion by the rush of streams from the

rocks

rocks that inclose it. Its profundity, though it should be such as is represented, can have little part in this exemption; for though deep wells are not frozen, because their water is secluded from the external air, yet where a wide surface is exposed to the full influence of a freezing atmosphere, I know not why the depth should keep it open. Natural philosophy is now one of the favourite studies of the Scottish nation, and *Lough Ness* well deserves to be diligently examined.

The road on which we travelled, and which was itself a source of entertainment, is made along the rock, in the direction of the lough, sometimes by breaking off protuberances, and sometimes by cutting the great mass of stone to a considerable depth. The fragments are piled in a loose wall on either side, with apertures left at very short spaces, to give a passage to the wintry currents. Part of it is bordered with low
trees,

trees, from which our guides gathered nuts, and would have had the appearance of an Englifh lane, except that an Englifh lane is almoft always dirty. It has been made with great labour, but has this advantage, that it cannot, without equal labour, be broken up.

Within our fight there were goats feeding or playing. The mountains have red deer, but they came not within view; and if what is faid of their vigilance and fubtlety be true, they have fome claim to that palm of wifdom, which the eaftern philofopher, whom Alexander interrogated, gave to thofe beafts which live furtheft from men.

Near the way, by the water fide, we efpied a cottage. This was the firft Highland Hut that I had feen; and as our bufinefs was with life and manners, we were willing to vifit it. To enter a habitation without leave, feems to be not confidered here

here as rudeness or intrusion. The old laws of hospitality still give this licence to a stranger.

A hut is constructed with loose stones, ranged for the most part with some tendency to circularity. It must be placed where the wind cannot act upon it with violence, because it has no cement; and where the water will run easily away, because it has no floor but the naked ground. The wall, which is commonly about six feet high, declines from the perpendicular a little inward. Such rafters as can be procured are then raised for a roof, and covered with heath, which makes a strong and warm thatch, kept from flying off by ropes of twisted heath, of which the ends, reaching from the centre of the thatch to the top of the wall, are held firm by the weight of a large stone. No light is admitted but at the entrance, and through a hole in the thatch, which gives vent to the smoke. This hole is not directly over the fire,

fire, left the rain should extinguish it; and the smoke therefore naturally fills the place before it escapes. Such is the general structure of the houses in which one of the nations of this opulent and powerful island has been hitherto content to live. Huts however are not more uniform than palaces; and this which we were inspecting was very far from one of the meanest, for it was divided into several apartments; and its inhabitants possessed such property as a pastoral poet might exalt into riches.

When we entered, we found an old woman boiling goats-flesh in a kettle. She spoke little English, but we had interpreters at hand; and she was willing enough to display her whole system of economy. She has five children, of which none are yet gone from her. The eldest, a boy of thirteen, and her husband, who is eighty years old, were at work in the wood. Her two next sons were gone to

Inverness to buy *meal*, by which oatmeal is always meant. Meal she considered as expensive food, and told us, that in Spring when the goats gave milk, the children could live without it. She is mistress of sixty goats, and I saw many kids in an enclosure at the end of her house. She had also some poultry. By the lake we saw a potatoe-garden, and a small spot of ground on which stood four shucks, containing each twelve sheaves of barley. She has all this from the labour of their own hands, and for what is necessary to be bought, her kids and her chickens are sent to market.

'With the true pastoral hospitality, she asked us to sit down and drink whisky. She is religious, and though the kirk is four miles off, probably eight English miles, she goes thither every Sunday. We gave her a shilling, and she begged snuff; for snuff is the luxury of a Highland cottage.

Soon

Soon afterwards we came to the *General's Hut*, so called because it was the temporary abode of Wade, while he superintended the works upon the road. It is now a house of entertainment for passengers, and we found it not ill stocked with provisions.

FALL OF FIERS.

Towards evening we crossed by a bridge, the river which makes the celebrated fall of Fiers. The country at the bridge strikes the imagination with all the gloom and grandeur of Siberian solitude. The way makes a flexure, and the mountains, covered with trees, rise at once on the left hand and in the front. We desired our guides to shew us the fall, and dismounting clambered over very rugged craggs, till I began to wish that our curiosity might have been gratified with less trouble and danger. We came at last to a place where we could overlook the river, and saw a channel torn, as it seems, through black piles of stone, by which the stream is obstructed and broken, till it comes to a very steep descent, of such dreadful depth, that we were naturally inclined to turn aside our eyes.

But we visited the place at an unseasonable time, and found it divested of its dignity and terror. Nature never gives every thing at once. A long continuance of dry weather, which made the rest of the way easy and delightful, deprived us of the pleasure expected from the fall of Fiers. The river having now no water but what the springs supply, showed us only a swift current, clear and shallow, fretting over the asperities of the rocky bottom, and we were left to exercise our thoughts, by endeavouring to conceive the effect of a thousand streams poured from the mountains into one channel, struggling for expansion in a narrow passage, exasperated by rocks rising in their way, and

at

at last discharging all their violence of waters by a sudden fall through the horrid chasm.

The way now grew less easy, descending by an uneven declivity, but without either dirt or danger. We did not arrive at Fort Augustus till it was late. Mr. *Boswell*, who, between his father's merit and his own, is sure of reception wherever he comes, sent a servant before to beg admission and entertainment for that night. Mr. Trapaud, the governor, treated us with that courtesy which is so closely connected with the military character. He came out to meet us beyond the gates, and apologized that, at so late an hour, the rules of a garrison suffered him to give us entrance only at the postern.

FORT AUGUSTUS.

In the morning we viewed the fort, which is much less than that of *St. George*,

and

and is said to be commanded by the neighbouring hills. It was not long ago taken by the Highlanders. But its situation seems well chosen for pleasure, if not for strength; it stands at the head of the lake, and, by a sloop of sixty tuns, is supplied from Inverness with great convenience.

We were now to cross the Highlands towards the western coast, and to content ourselves with such accommodations, as a way so little frequented could afford. The journey was not formidable, for it was but of two days, very unequally divided, because the only house, where we could be entertained, was not further off than a third of the way. We soon came to a high hill, which we mounted by a military road, cut in traverses, so that as we went upon a higher stage, we saw the baggage following us below in a contrary direction. To make this way, the rock has been hewn to a level with labour that might have broken

broken the perseverance of a Roman legion.

The country is totally denuded of its wood, but the stumps both of oaks and firs, which are still found, shew that it has been once a forest of large timber. I do not remember that we saw any animals, but we were told that, in the mountains, there are stags, roebucks, goats, and rabbits.

We did not perceive that this tract was possessed by human beings, except that once we saw a corn-field, in which a lady was walking with some gentlemen. Their house was certainly at no great distance, but so situated that we could not descry it.

Passing on through the dreariness of solitude, we found a party of soldiers from the fort, working on the road, under the superintendence of a serjeant. We told them

them how kindly we had been treated at the garrison, and as we were enjoying the benefit of their labours, begged leave to shew our gratitude by a small present.

ANOCH.

Early in the afternoon we came to Anoch, a village in *Glenmollison* of three huts, one of which is distinguished by a chimney. Here we were to dine and lodge, and were conducted through the first room, that had the chimney, into another lighted by a small glass window. The landlord attended us with great civility, and told us what he could give us to eat and drink. I found some books on a shelf, among which were a volume or more of Prideaux's Connection.

This I mentioned as something unexpected, and perceived that I did not please him. I praised the propriety of his language,

guage, and was anfwered that I need not wonder, for he had learned it by grammar.

By fubfequent opportunities of obfervation I found that my hoft's diction had nothing peculiar. Thofe Highlanders that can fpeak Englifh, commonly fpeak it well, with few of the words, and little of the tone by which a Scotchman is diftinguifhed. Their language feems to have been learned in the army or the navy, or by fome communication with thofe who could give them good examples of accent and pronunciation. By their Lowland neighbours they would not willingly be taught; for they have long confidered them as a mean and degenerate race. Thefe prejudices are wearing faft away; but fo much of them ftill remains, that when I afked a very learned minifter in the iflands, which they confidered as their moft favage clans: " *Thofe*, faid he, *that live next the Low-* " *lands.*"

As we came hither early in the day, we had time sufficient to survey the place. The house was built like other huts of loose stones, but the part in which we dined and slept was lined with turf and wattled with twigs, which kept the earth from falling. Near it was a garden of turnips and a field of potatoes. It stands in a glen, or valley, pleasantly watered by a winding river. But this country, however it may delight the gazer or amuse the naturalist, is of no great advantage to its owners. Our landlord told us of a gentleman, who possesses lands, eighteen Scotch miles in length, and three in breadth; a space containing at least a hundred square English miles. He has raised his rents to the danger of depopulating his farms, and he fells his timber, and by exerting every art of augmentation, has obtained an yearly revenue of four hundred pounds, which for a hundred

hundred square miles is three half-pence an acre.

Some time after dinner we were surprised by the entrance of a young woman, not inelegant either in mien or dress, who asked us whether we would have tea. We found that she was the daughter of our host, and desired her to make it. Her conversation, like her appearance, was gentle and pleasing. We knew that the girls of the Highlands are all gentlewomen, and treated her with great respect, which she received as customary and due, and was neither elated by it, nor confused, but repaid my civilities without embarrassment, and told me how much I honoured her country by coming to survey it.

She had been at *Inverness* to gain the common female qualifications, and had, like her father, the English pronunciation. I presented her with a book, which I happened

pened to have about me, and should not be pleased to think that she forgets me.

In the evening the soldiers, whom we had passed on the road, came to spend at our inn the little money that we had given them. They had the true military impatience of coin in their pockets, and had marched at least six miles to find the first place where liquor could be bought. Having never been before in a place so wild and unfrequented, I was glad of their arrival, because I knew that we had made them friends, and to gain still more of their good will, we went to them, where they were carousing in the barn, and added something to our former gift. All that we gave was not much, but it detained them in the barn, either merry or quarrelling, the whole night, and in the morning they went back to their work, with great indignation at the bad qualities of whisky.

We

We had gained so much the favour of our host, that when we left his house in the morning, he walked by us a great way, and entertained us with conversation both on his own condition, and that of the country. His life seemed to be merely pastoral, except that he differed from some of the ancient Nomades in having a settled dwelling. His wealth consists of one hundred sheep, as many goats, twelve milk-cows, and twenty-eight beeves ready for the drovers.

From him we first heard of the general dissatisfaction, which is now driving the Highlanders into the other hemisphere; and when I asked him whether they would stay at home, if they were well treated, he answered with indignation, that no man willingly left his native country. Of the farm, which he himself occupied, the rent had, in twenty-five years, been advanced from five to twenty pounds, which he

found

found himself so little able to pay, that he would be glad to try his fortune in some other place. Yet he owned the reasonableness of raising the Highland rents in a certain degree, and declared himself willing to pay ten pounds for the ground which he had formerly had for five.

Our host having amused us for a time, resigned us to our guides. The journey of this day was long, not that the distance was great, but that the way was difficult. We were now in the bosom of the Highlands, with full leisure to contemplate the appearance and properties of mountainous regions, such as have been, in many countries, the last shelters of national distress, and are every where the scenes of adventures, stratagems, surprises, and escapes.

Mountainous countries are not passed but with difficulty, not merely from the labour

labour of climbing; for to climb is not always neceſſary: but becauſe that which is not mountain is commonly bog, through which the way muſt be picked with caution. Where there are hills, there is much rain, and the torrents pouring down into the intermediate ſpaces, ſeldom find ſo ready an outlet, as not to ſtagnate till they have broken the texture of the ground.

Of the hills, which our journey offered to the view on either ſide, we did not take the height, nor did we ſee any that aſtoniſhed us with their loftineſs. Towards the ſummit of one, there was a white ſpot, which I ſhould have called a naked rock, but the guides, who had better eyes, and were acquainted with the phænomena of the country, declared it to be ſnow. It had already laſted to the end of Auguſt, and was likely to maintain its conteſt with the ſun, till it ſhould be reinforced by winter.

The

The height of mountains philosophically considered is properly computed from the surface of the next sea; but as it affects the eye or imagination of the passenger, as it makes either a spectacle or an obstruction, it must be reckoned from the place where the rise begins to make a considerable angle with the plain. In extensive continents the land may, by gradual elevation, attain great height, without any other appearance than that of a plane gently inclined, and if a hill placed upon such raised ground be described, as having its altitude equal to the whole space above the sea, the representation will be fallacious.

These mountains may be properly enough measured from the inland base; for it is not much above the sea. As we advanced at evening towards the western coast, I did not observe the declivity to be greater than

than is neceffary for the difcharge of the inland waters.

We paffed many rivers and rivulets, which commonly ran with a clear fhallow ftream over a hard pebbly bottom. Thefe channels, which feem fo much wider than the water that they convey would naturally require, are formed by the violence of wintry floods, produced by the accumulation of innumerable ftreams that fall in rainy weather from the hills, and burfting away with refiftlefs impetuofity, make themfelves a paffage proportionate to their mafs.

Such capricious and temporary waters cannot be expected to produce many fifh. The rapidity of the wintry deluge fweeps them away, and the fcantinefs of the fummer ftream would hardly fuftain them above the ground. This is the reafon why in fording the northern rivers, no fishes are seen, as in England, wandering in the water.

Of the hills many may be called with Homer's Ida *abundant in springs*, but few can deserve the epithet which he bestows upon Pelion by *waving their leaves*. They exhibit very little variety; being almost wholly covered with dark heath, and even that seems to be checked in its growth. What is not heath is nakedness, a little diversified by now and then a stream rushing down the steep. An eye accustomed to flowery pastures and waving harvests is astonished and repelled by this wide extent of hopeless sterility. The appearance is that of matter incapable of form or usefulness, dismissed by nature from her care and disinherited of her favours, left in its original elemental state, or quickened only with one sullen power of useless vegetation.

It

It will very readily occur, that this uniformity of barrenness can afford very little amusement to the traveller; that it is easy to sit at home and conceive rocks and heath, and waterfalls; and that these journeys are useless labours, which neither impregnate the imagination, nor enlarge the understanding. It is true that of far the greater part of things, we must content ourselves with such knowledge as description may exhibit, or analogy supply; but it is true likewise, that these ideas are always incomplete, and that at least, till we have compared them with realities, we do not know them to be just. As we see more, we become possessed of more certainties, and consequently gain more principles of reasoning, and found a wider basis of analogy.

Regions mountainous and wild, thinly inhabited, and little cultivated, make a great part of the earth, and he that has never seen them, must live unacquainted with much of the face of nature, and with one of the great scenes of human existence.

As the day advanced towards noon, we entered a narrow valley not very flowery, but sufficiently verdant. Our guides told us, that the horses could not travel all day without rest or meat, and entreated us to stop here, because no grass would be found in any other place. The request was reasonable and the argument cogent. We therefore willingly dismounted and diverted ourselves as the place gave us opportunity.

I sat down on a bank, such as a writer of Romance might have delighted to feign. I had indeed no trees to whisper over my head, but a clear rivulet streamed at my my feet. The day was calm, the air foft, and all was rudenefs, filence, and folitude. Before me, and on either fide, were high hills, which by hindering the eye from ranging, forced the mind to find entertainment for itfelf. Whether I fpent the hour well I know not; for here I firft conceived the thought of this narration.

We were in this place at eafe and by choice, and had no evils to fuffer or to fear; yet the imaginations excited by the view of an unknown and untravelled wildernefs are not fuch as arife in the artificial folitude of parks and gardens; a flattering notion of felf-fufficiency, a placid indulgence of voluntary delufions, a fecure expanfion of the fancy, or a cool concentration of the mental powers. The phantoms which haunt a defert are want, and mifery, and danger; the evils of dereliction rufh upon the thoughts; man is

made

made unwillingly acquainted with his own weakneſs, and meditation ſhews him only how little he can ſuſtain, and how little he can perform. There were no traces of inhabitants, except perhaps a rude pile of clods called a ſummer hut, in which a herdſman had reſted in the favourable ſeaſons. Whoever had been in the place where I then ſat, unprovided with proviſions and ignorant of the country, might, at leaſt before the roads were made, have wandered among the rocks, till he had periſhed with hardſhip, before he could have found either food or ſhelter. Yet what are theſe hillocks to the ridges of Taurus, or theſe ſpots of wildneſs to the deſarts of America?

It was not long before we were invited to mount, and continued our journey along the ſide of a lough, kept full by many ſtreams, which with more or leſs rapidity and noiſe croſſed the road from the hills on the other hand. These currents, in their diminished state, after several dry months, afford, to one who has always lived in level countries, an unusual and delightful spectacle; but in the rainy season, such as every winter may be expected to bring, must precipitate an impetuous and tremendous flood. I suppose the way by which we went, is at that time impassable.

GLENSHEALS.

The lough at last ended in a river broad and shallow like the rest, but that it may be passed when it is deeper, there is a bridge over it. Beyond it is a valley called *Glensheals*, inhabited by the clan of Macrae. Here we found a village called *Auknasheals*, consisting of many huts, perhaps twenty, built all of *dry-stone*, that is, stones piled up without mortar,

We

We had, by the direction of the officers at Fort *Augustus*, taken bread for ourselves, and tobacco for those Highlanders who might shew us any kindness. We were now at a place where we could obtain milk, but must have wanted bread if we had not brought it. The people of this valley did not appear to know any English, and our guides now became doubly necessary as interpreters. A woman, whose hut was distinguished by greater spaciousness and better architecture, brought out some pails of milk. The villagers gathered about us in considerable numbers, I believe without any evil intention, but with a very savage wildness of aspect and manner. When our meal was over, Mr. *Boswell* sliced the bread, and divided it amongst them, as he supposed them never to have tasted a wheaten loaf before. He then gave them little pieces of twisted tobacco, and among the children we distributed a small handful of halfpence, which they received with great

great eagerness. Yet I have been since told, that the people of that valley are not indigent; and when we mentioned them afterwards as needy and pitiable, a Highland lady let us know, that we might spare our commiseration; for the dame whose milk we drank had probably more than a dozen milk-cows. She seemed unwilling to take any price, but being pressed to make a demand, at last named a shilling. Honesty is not greater where elegance is less. One of the by-standers, as we were told afterwards, advised her to ask more, but she said a shilling was enough. We gave her half a crown, and I hope got some credit by our behaviour; for the company said, if our interpreters did not flatter us, that they had not seen such a day since the old laird of Macleod passed through their country.

The Macraes, as we heard afterwards in the Hebrides, were originally an indigent and

and subordinate clan, and having no farms nor stock, were in great numbers servants to the Maclellans, who, in the war of Charles the First, took arms at the call of the heroic *Montrose*, and were, in one of his battles, almost all destroyed. The women that were left at home, being thus deprived of their husbands, like the Scythian ladies of old, married their servants, and the Macraes became a considerable race.

THE HIGHLANDS.

As we continued our journey, we were at leisure to extend our speculations, and to investigate the reason of those peculiarities by which such rugged regions as these before us are generally distinguished.

Mountainous countries commonly contain the original, at least the oldest race of inhabitants, for they are not easily conquered,

quered, becaufe they muft be entered by narrow ways, expofed to every power of mifchief from thofe that occupy the heights; and every new ridge is a new fortrefs, where the defendants have again the fame advantages. If the affailants either force the ftrait, or ftorm the fummit, they gain only fo much ground; their enemies are fled to take poffeffion of the next rock, and the purfuers ftand at gaze, knowing neither where the ways of efcape wind among the fteeps, nor where the bog has firmnefs to fuftain them: befides that, mountaineers have an agility in climbing and defcending diftinct from ftrength or courage, and attainable only by ufe.

If the war be not foon concluded, the invaders are diflodged by hunger; for in thofe anxious and toilfome marches, provifions cannot eafily be carried, and are never to be found. The wealth of mountains is cattle, which, while the men ftand in the paffes, the women drive away.

Such

Such lands at last cannot repay the expence of conquest, and therefore perhaps have not been so often invaded by the mere ambition of dominion; as by resentment of robberies and insults, or the desire of enjoying in security the more fruitful provinces.

As mountains are long before they are conquered, they are likewise long before they are civilized. Men are softened by intercourse mutually profitable, and instructed by comparing their own notions with those of others. Thus Cæsar found the maritime parts of Britain made less barbarous by their commerce with the Gauls. Into a barren and rough tract no stranger is brought either by the hope of gain or of pleasure. The inhabitants having neither commodities for sale, nor money for purchase, seldom visit more polished places, or if they do visit them seldom return.

It

It sometimes happens that by conquest, intermixture, or gradual refinement, the cultivated parts of a country change their language. The mountaineers then become a distinct nation, cut off by dissimilitude of speech from conversation with their neighbours. Thus in Biscay, the original Cantabrian, and in Dalecarlia, the old Swedish still subsists. Thus Wales and the Highlands speak the tongue of the first inhabitants of Britain, while the other parts have received first the Saxon, and in some degree afterwards the French, and then formed a third language between them.

That the primitive manners are continued where the primitive language is spoken, no nation will desire me to suppose, for the manners of mountaineers are commonly savage, but they are rather produced by their situation than derived from their ancestors.

Such

Such seems to be the disposition of man, that whatever makes a distinction produces rivalry. England, before other causes of enmity were found, was disturbed for some centuries by the contests of the northern and southern counties; so that at Oxford, the peace of study could for a long time be preserved only by chusing annually one of the proctors from each side of the Trent. A tract intersected by many ridges of mountains, naturally divides its inhabitants into petty nations, which are made by a thousand causes enemies to each other. Each will exalt its own chiefs, each will boast the valour of its men, or the beauty of its women, and every claim of superiority irritates competition; injuries will sometimes be done, and be more injuriously defended; retaliation will sometimes be attempted, and the debt exacted with too much interest.

In the Highlands it was a law, that if a robber was sheltered from justice, any man of the same clan might be taken in his place. This was a kind of irregular justice, which, though necessary in savage times, could hardly fail to end in a feud, and a feud once kindled among an idle people with no variety of pursuits to divert their thoughts, burnt on for ages either sullenly glowing in secret mischief, or openly blazing into public violence. Of the effects of this violent judicature, there are not wanting memorials. The cave is now to be seen to which one of the Campbells, who had injured the Macdonalds, retired with a body of his own clan. The Macdonalds required the offender, and being refused, made a fire at the mouth of the cave, by which he and his adherents were suffocated together.

Mountaineers are warlike, because by their feuds and competitions they consider themselves as surrounded with enemies, and are always prepared to repel incursions, or to make them. Like the Greeks in their unpolifhed ftate, defcribed by Thucydides, the Highlanders, till lately, went always armed, and carried their weapons to vifits, and to church.

Mountaineers are thievifh, becaufe they are poor, and having neither manufactures nor commerce, can grow richer only by robbery. They regularly plunder their neighbours, for their neighbours are commonly their enemies; and having loft that reverence for property, by which the order of civil life is preferved, foon confider all as enemies, whom they do not reckon as friends, and think themfelves licenfed to invade whatever they are not obliged to protect.

By a ftrict adminiftration of the laws, fince the laws have been introduced into the Highlands, this difpofition to thievery is very much repreft. Thirty years ago no

herd

herd had ever been conducted through the mountains, without paying tribute in the night to some of the clans; but cattle are now driven, and passengers travel without danger, fear, or molestation.

Among a warlike people, the quality of highest esteem is personal courage, and with the ostentatious display of courage are closely connected promptitude of offence and quickness of resentment. The Highlanders, before they were disarmed, were so addicted to quarrels, that the boys used to follow any publick procession or ceremony, however festive, or however solemn, in expectation of the battle, which was sure to happen before the company dispersed.

Mountainous regions are sometimes so remote from the seat of government, and so difficult of access, that they are very little under the influence of the sovereign, or within the reach of national justice. Law is nothing without power; and the sentence of a distant court could not be easily executed, nor perhaps very safely promulgated, among men ignorantly proud and habitually violent, unconnected with the general system, and accustomed to reverence only their own lords. It has therefore been necessary to erect many particular jurisdictions, and commit the punishment of crimes, and the decision of right to the proprietors of the country who could enforce their own decrees. It immediately appears that such judges will be often ignorant, and often partial; but in the immaturity of political establishments no better expedient could be found. As government advances towards perfection, provincial judicature is perhaps in every empire gradually abolished.

Those who had thus the dispensation of law, were by consequence themselves lawless.

lefs. Their vaffals had no fhelter from outrages and oppreffions; but were condemned to endure, without refiftance, the caprices of wantonnefs, and the rage of cruelty.

In the Highlands, fome great lords had an hereditary jurifdiction over counties; and fome chieftains over their own lands; till the final conqueft of the Highlands afforded an opportunity of crufhing all the local courts, and of extending the general benefits of equal law to the low and the high, in the deepeft recefses and obfcureft corners.

While the chiefs had this refemblance of royalty, they had little inclination to appeal, on any queftion, to fuperior judicatures. A claim of lands between two powerful lairds was decided like a conteft for dominion between fovereign powers. They drew their forces into the field, and right attended on the ftrongeft. This was, in ruder times, the common practice, which the kings of Scotland could feldom control.

Even fo lately as in the laft years of King William, a battle was fought at *Mull Roy*, on a plain a few miles to the fouth of *Invernefs*, between the clans of *Mackintofh* and *Macdonald* of *Keppoch*. Col. *Macdonald*, the head of a fmall clan, refufed to pay the dues demanded from him by *Mackintofh*, as his fuperior lord. They difdained the interpofition of judges and laws, and calling each his followers to maintain the dignity of the clan, fought a formal battle, in which feveral confiderable men fell on the fide of *Mackintofh*, without a complete victory to either. This is faid to have been the laft open war made between the clans by their own authority.

The Highland lords made treaties, and formed alliances, of which fome traces may
ftill

still be found, and some consequences still remain as lasting evidences of petty regality. The terms of one of these confederacies were, that each should support the other in the right, or in the wrong, except against the king.

The inhabitants of mountains form distinct races, and are careful to preserve their genealogies. Men in a small district necessarily mingle blood by intermarriages, and combine at last into one family, with a common interest in the honour and disgrace of every individual. Then begins that union of affections, and co-operation of endeavours, that constitute a clan. They who consider themselves as ennobled by their family, will think highly of their progenitors, and they who through successive generations live always together in the same place, will preserve local stories and hereditary prejudices. Thus every Highlander can talk of his ancestors, and recount the outrages which they suffered from the wicked inhabitants of the next valley.

Such are the effects of habitation among mountains, and such were the qualities of the Highlanders, while their rocks secluded them from the rest of mankind, and kept them an unaltered and discriminated race. They are now losing their distinction, and hastening to mingle with the general community.

GLENELG.

We left *Auknasheals* and the *Macraes* in the afternoon, and in the evening came to *Ratiken*, a high hill on which a road is cut, but so steep and narrow, that it is very difficult. There is now a design of making another way round the bottom. Upon one of the precipices, my horse, weary with the steepness of the rise, staggered a little, and

and I called in haſte to the Highlander to hold him. This was the only moment of my journey, in which I thought myſelf endangered.

Having ſurmounted the hill at laſt, we were told that at *Glenelg*, on the ſea-ſide, we ſhould come to a houſe of lime and ſlate and glaſs. This image of magnificence raiſed our expectation. At laſt we came to our inn weary and peeviſh, and began to inquire for meat and beds,

Of the proviſions the negative catalogue was very copious. Here was no meat, no milk, no bread, no eggs, no wine. We did not expreſs much ſatisfaction. Here however we were to ſtay. Whiſky we might have, and I believe at laſt they caught a fowl and killed it. We had ſome bread, and with that we prepared ourſelves to be contented, when we had a very eminent proof of Highland hoſpitality. Along some miles of the way, in the evening, a gentleman's servant had kept us company on foot with very little notice on our part. He left us near *Glenelg*, and we thought on him no more till he came to us again, in about two hours, with a present from his master of rum and sugar. The man had mentioned his company, and the gentleman, whose name, I think, is *Gordon*, well knowing the penury of the place, had this attention to two men, whose names perhaps he had not heard, by whom his kindness was not likely to be ever repaid, and who could be recommended to him him only by their necessities.

We were now to examine our lodging. Out of one of the beds, on which we were to repose, started up, at our entrance, a man black as a Cyclops from the forge. Other circumstances of no elegant recital concurred to disgust us. We had been frighted by a lady at Edinburgh, with discouraging

discouraging reprefentations of Highland lodgings. Sleep, however, was neceffary. Our Highlanders had at laft found fome hay, with which the inn could not fupply them. I directed them to bring a bundle into the room, and flept upon it in my riding coat. Mr. Bofwell being more delicate, laid himfelf fheets with hay over and under him, and lay in linen like a gentleman.

SKY. ARMYDEL.

In the morning, September the twentieth, we found ourfelves on the edge of the fea. Having procured a boat, we difmiffed our Highlanders, whom I would recommend to the fervice of any future travellers, and were ferried over to the ifle of Sky. We landed at *Armidel*, where we were met on the fands by Sir Alexander Macdonald, who was at that time there with his lady, preparing to leave the ifland and refide at Edinburgh.

Armidel is a neat house, built where the *Macdonalds* had once a seat, which was burnt in the commotions that followed the Revolution. The walled orchard, which belonged to the former house, still remains. It is well shaded by tall ash trees, of a species, as Mr. Janes the fossilist informed me, uncommonly valuable. This plantation is very properly mentioned by Dr. *Campbell*, in his new account of the state of *Britain*, and deserves attention; because it proves that the present nakedness of the *Hebrides* is not wholly the fault of nature.

As we sat at Sir Alexander's table, we were entertained, according to the ancient usage of the North, with the melody of the bagpipe. Every thing in those countries has its history. As the bagpiper was playing, an elderly gentleman informed us, that in some remote time, the *Macdonalds* of Glengary having been injured, or offended by the inhabitants of *Culloden*, and

and refolving to have juftice or vengeance, came to *Culloden* on a Sunday, where finding their enemies at worfhip, they fhut them up in the church, which they fet on fire; and this, faid he, is the tune that the piper played while they were burning.

Narrations like this, however uncertain, deferve the notice of a traveller, becaufe they are the only records of a nation that has no hiftorians, and afford the moft genuine reprefentation of the life and character of the ancient Highlanders.

Under the denomination of *Highlander* are comprehended in Scotland all that now fpeak the Erfe language, or retain the primitive manners, whether they live among the mountains or in the iflands; and in that fenfe I ufe the name, when there is not fome apparent reafon for making a diftinction.

In *Sky* I first observed the use of Brogues, a kind of artless shoes, stitched with thongs so loosely, that though they defend the foot from stones, they do not exclude water. Brogues were formerly made of raw hides, with the hair inwards, and such are perhaps still used in rude and remote parts; but they are said not to last above two days. Where life is somewhat improved, they are now made of leather tanned with oak bark, as in other places, or with the bark of birch, or roots of tormentil, a substance recommended in defect of bark, about forty years ago, to the Irish tanners, by one to whom the parliament of that kingdom voted a reward. The leather of *Sky* is not completely penetrated by vegetable matter, and therefore cannot be very durable.

My inquiries about brogues, gave me an early specimen of Highland information.

tion. One day I was told, that to make brogues was a domeſtic art, which every man practiſed for himſelf, and that a pair of brogues was the work of an hour. I ſuppoſed that the huſband made brogues as the wife made an apron, till next day it was told me, that a brogue-maker was a trade, and that a pair would coſt half a crown. It will eaſily occur that theſe re-preſentations may both be true, and that, in ſome places, men may buy them, and in others, make them for themſelves; but I had both the accounts in the ſame houſe within two days.

Many of my ſubſequent inquiries upon more intereſting topicks ended in the like uncertainty. He that travels in the Highlands may eaſily ſaturate his ſoul with intelligence, if he will acquieſce in the firſt account. The Highlander gives to every queſtion an anſwer ſo prompt and peremptory, that ſkepticiſm itſelf is dared into ſilence,

silence, and the mind sinks before the bold reporter in unresisting credulity; but if a second question be ventured, it breaks the enchantment; for it is immediately discovered, that what was told so confidently was told at hazard, and that such fearlessness of assertion was either the sport of negligence, or the refuge of ignorance.

If individuals are thus at variance with themselves, it can be no wonder that the accounts of different men are contradictory. The traditions of an ignorant and savage people have been for ages negligently heard, and unskilfully related. Distant events must have been mingled together, and the actions of one man given to another. These, however, are deficiencies in story, for which no man is now to be censured. It were enough, if what there is yet opportunity of examining were accurately inspected, and justly represented; but such is the laxity of Highland conversation, that the

the inquirer is kept in continual suspense, and by a kind of intellectual retrogradation, knows less as he hears more.

In the islands the plaid is rarely worn. The law by which the Highlanders have been obliged to change the form of their dress, has, in all the places that we have visited, been universally obeyed. I have seen only one gentleman completely clothed in the ancient habit, and by him it was worn only occasionally and wantonly. The common people do not think themselves under any legal necessity of having coats; for they say that the law against plaids was made by Lord Hardwicke, and was in force only for his life: but the same poverty that made it then difficult for them to change their clothing, hinders them now from changing it again.

The fillibeg, or lower garment, is still very common, and the bonnet almost universal;

versal; but their attire is such as produces, in a sufficient degree, the effect intended by the law, of abolishing the dissimilitude of appearance between the Highlanders and the other inhabitants of Britain; and, if dress be supposed to have much influence, facilitates their coalition with their fellow-subjects.

What we have long used we naturally like, and therefore the Highlanders were unwilling to lay aside their plaid, which yet to an unprejudiced spectator must appear an incommodious and cumbersome dress; for, hanging loose upon the body, it must flutter in a quick motion, or require one of the hands to keep it close. The Romans always laid aside the gown when they had any thing to do. It was a dress so unsuitable to war, that the same word which signified a gown signified peace. The chief use of a plaid seems to be this, that they could commodiously wrap themselves in it,
when

when they were obliged to sleep without a better cover.

In our passage from *Scotland* to *Sky*, we were wet for the first time with a shower. This was the beginning of the Highland winter, after which we were told that a succession of three dry days was not to be expected for many months. The winter of the *Hebrides* consists of little more than rain and wind. As they are surrounded by an ocean never frozen, the blasts that come to them over the water are too much softened to have the power of congelation. The salt loughs, or inlets of the sea, which shoot very far into the island, never have any ice upon them; and the pools of fresh water will never bear the walker. The snow that sometimes falls, is soon dissolved by the air, or the rain.

This is not the description of a cruel climate, yet the dark months are here a time of great distress; because the summer can do little more than feed itself, and winter comes with its cold and its scarcity upon families very slenderly provided.

CORIATACHAN IN SKY.

The third or fourth day after our arrival at *Armidel*, brought us an invitation to the isle of *Raasay*, which lies east of *Sky*. It is incredible how soon the account of any event is propagated in these narrow countries by the love of talk, which much leisure produces, and the relief given to the mind in the penury of insular conversation by a new topick. The arrival of strangers at a place so rarely visited, excites rumour, and quickens curiosity. I know not whether we touched at any corner, where Fame had not already prepared us a reception.

To gain a commodious passage to *Raasay*, it was necessary to pass over a large part of *Sky*.

Sky. We were furnished therefore with horses and a guide. In the islands there are no roads, nor any marks by which a stranger may find his way. The horseman has always at his side a native of the place, who, by pursuing game, or tending cattle, or being often employed in messages or conduct, has learned where the ridge of the hill has breadth sufficient to allow a horse and his rider a passage, and where the moss or bog is hard enough to bear them. The bogs are avoided as toilsome at least, if not unsafe, and therefore the journey is made generally from precipice to precipice; from which if the eye ventures to look down, it sees below a gloomy cavity, whence the rush of water is sometimes heard.

But there seems to be in all this more alarm than danger. The Highlander walks carefully before, and the horse, accustomed to the ground, follows him with little deviation. Sometimes the hill is too steep for the horseman to keep his seat, and sometimes the moss is too tremulous to bear the double weight of horse and man. The rider then dismounts, and all shift as they can.

Journies made in this manner are rather tedious than long. A very few miles require several hours. From *Armidel* we came at night to *Coriatachan*, a house very pleasantly situated between two brooks, with one of the highest hills of the island behind it. It is the residence of Mr. *Mackinnon*, by whom we were treated with very liberal hospitality, among a more numerous and elegant company than it could have been supposed easy to collect.

The hill behind the house we did not climb. The weather was rough, and the height and steepness discouraged us. We were told that there is a cairne upon it. A cairne is a heap of stones thrown upon the grave of one eminent for dignity of birth, or splendour of atchievements. It is said that by digging, an urn is always found under these cairnes: they must therefore have been thus piled by a people whose custom was to burn the dead. To pile stones is, I believe, a northern custom, and to burn the body was the Roman practice; nor do I know when it was that these two acts of sepulture were united.

The weather was next day too violent for the continuation of our journey; but we had no reason to complain of the interruption. We saw in every place, what we chiefly desired to know, the manners of the people. We had company, and, if we had chosen retirement, we might have had books.

I never was in any house of the Islands, where I did not find books in more languages than one, if I staid long enough to want them, except one from which the family was removed. Literature is not neglected by the higher rank of the Hebridians.

It need not, I suppose, be mentioned, that in countries so little frequented as the Islands, there are no houses where travellers are entertained for money. He that wanders about these wilds, either procures recommendations to those whose habitations lie near his way, or, when night and weariness come upon him, takes the chance of general hospitality. If he finds only a cottage, he can expect little more than shelter; for the cottagers have little more for themselves: but if his good fortune brings him to the residence of a gentleman, he will be glad of a storm to prolong his stay. There is, however, one inn by the sea-side at Sconsor, in Sky, where the post-office is kept.

At the tables where a stranger is received, neither plenty nor delicacy is wanting. A
tract

tract of land so thinly inhabited, must have much wild-fowl; and I scarcely remember to have seen a dinner without them. The moor-game is every where to be had. That the sea abounds with fish, needs not be told, for it supplies a great part of Europe. The isle of *Sky* has stags and roebucks, but no hares. They sell very numerous droves of oxen yearly to England, and therefore cannot be supposed to want beef at home. Sheep and goats are in great numbers, and they have the common domestick fowls.

But as here is nothing to be bought, every family must kill its own meat, and roast part of it somewhat sooner than Apicius would prescribe. Every kind of flesh is undoubtedly excelled by the variety and emulation of English markets; but that which is not best may be yet very free from bad, and he that shall complain of his fare in the *Hebrides*, has improved his delicacy more than his manhood.

Their fowls are not like those plumped for sale by the poulterers of London, but they are as good as other places commonly afford, except that the geese, by feeding in the sea, have universally a fishy rankness.

These geese seem to be of a middle race, between the wild and domestick kinds. They are so tame as to own a home, and so wild as sometimes to fly quite away.

Their native bread is made of oats, or barley. Of oatmeal they spread very thin cakes, coarse and hard, to which unaccustomed palates are not easily reconciled. The barley cakes are thicker and softer; I began to eat them without unwillingness; the blackness of their colour raises some dislike, but the taste is not disagreeable.

In

In most houses there is wheat flower, with which we were sure to be treated, if we staid long enough to have it kneaded and baked. As neither yeast nor leaven are used among them, their bread of every kind is unfermented. They make only cakes, and never mould a loaf.

A man of the Hebrides, for of the women's diet I can give no account, as soon as he appears in the morning, swallows a glass of whisky; yet they are not a drunken race, at least I never was present at much intemperance; but no man is so abstemious as to refuse the morning dram, which they call a *skalk*.

The word *whisky* signifies water, and is applied by way of eminence to *strong water*, or distilled liquor. The spirit drunk in the North is drawn from barley. I never tasted it, except once for experiment at the inn in *Inverary*, when I thought it preferable

ferable to any *English* malt brandy. It was strong, but not pungent, and was free from the empyreumatic taste or smell. What was the process I had no opportunity of inquiring, nor do I wish to improve the art of making poison pleasant.

Not long after the dram, may be expected the breakfast, a meal in which the Scots, whether of the lowlands or mountains, must be confessed to excel us. The tea and coffee are accompanied not only with butter, but with honey, conserves, and marmalades. If an epicure could remove by a wish, in quest of sensual gratifications, wherever he had supped he would breakfast in Scotland.

In the islands, however, they do what I found it not very easy to endure. They pollute the tea-table by plates piled with large slices of Cheshire cheese, which mingles its less grateful odours with the fragrance of the tea.

Where

Where many questions are to be asked, some will be omitted. I forgot to enquire how they were supplied with so much exotic luxury. Perhaps the French may bring them wine for wool, and the Dutch give them tea and coffee at the fishing season, in exchange for fresh provision. Their trade is unconstrained; they pay no customs; for there is no officer to demand them; whatever therefore is made dear only by impost, is obtained here at an easy rate.

A dinner in the Western Islands differs very little from a dinner in *England*, except that in the place of tarts, there are always set different preparations of milk. This part of their diet will admit some improvement. Though they have milk, and eggs, and sugar, few of them know how to compound them in a custard. Their gardens afford them no great variety, but they have always some vegetables on the table.

table. Potatoes at leaſt are never wanting, which, though they have not known them long, are now one of the principal parts of their food. They are not of the mealy, but the viſcous kind.

Their more elaborate cookery, or made diſhes, an Engliſhman, at the firſt taſte is not likely to approve, but the culinary compoſitions of every country are often ſuch as become grateful to other nations only by degrees; though I have read a French author, who, in the elation of his heart, ſays, that French cookery pleaſes all foreigners, but foreign cookery never ſatisfies a Frenchman.

Their ſuppers are, like their dinners, various and plentiful. The table is always covered with elegant linen. Their plates for common uſe are often of that kind of manufacture which is called cream coloured, or queen's ware. They uſe ſilver on all occasions where it is common in *England*, nor did I ever find the spoon of horn, but in one house.

The knives are not often either very bright, or very sharp. They are indeed instruments of which the Highlanders have not been long acquainted with the general use. They were not regularly laid on the table, before the prohibition of arms, and the change of dress. Thirty years ago the Highlander wore his knife as a companion to his dirk or dagger, and when the company sat down to meat, the men who had knives, cut the flesh into small pieces for the women, who with their fingers conveyed it to their mouths.

There was perhaps never any change of national manners so quick, so great, and so general, as that which has operated in the Highlands, by the last conquest, and the subsequent laws. We came thither
too

too late to see what we expected, a people of peculiar appearance, and a system of antiquated life. The clans retain little now of their original character, their ferocity of temper is softened, their military ardour is extinguished, their dignity of independence is depressed, their contempt of government subdued, and their reverence for their chiefs abated. Of what they had before the late conquest of their country, there remain only their language and their poverty. Their language is attacked on every side. Schools are erected, in which *English* only is taught, and there were lately some who thought it reasonable to refuse them a version of the holy scriptures, that they might have no monument of their mother-tongue.

That their poverty is gradually abated, cannot be mentioned among the unpleasing consequences of subjection. They are now acquainted with money, and the possibility of of gain will by degrees make them induſtrious. Such is the effect of the late regulations, that a longer journey than to the Highlands muſt be taken by him whoſe curioſity pants for ſavage virtues and barbarous grandeur.

RAASAY.

At the firſt intermiſſion of the ſtormy weather we were informed, that the boat, which was to convey us to *Raaſay*, attended us on the coaſt. We had from this time our intelligence facilitated, and our converſation enlarged, by the company of Mr. *Macqueen*, miniſter of a pariſh in *Sky*, whoſe knowledge and politeneſs give him a title equally to kindneſs and reſpect, and who, from this time, never forſook us till we were preparing to leave *Sky*, and the adjacent places.

The boat was under the direction of Mr. *Malcolm Macleod*, a gentleman of *Raaſay*.

asay. The water was calm, and the rowers were vigorous; so that our passage was quick and pleasant. When we came near the island, we saw the laird's house, a neat modern fabrick, and found Mr. *Macleod*, the proprietor of the Island, with many gentlemen, expecting us on the beach. We had, as at all other places, some difficulty in landing. The crags were irregularly broken, and a false step would have been very mischievous.

It seemed that the rocks might, with no great labour, have been hewn almost into a regular flight of steps; and as there are no other landing places, I considered this rugged ascent as the consequence of a form of life inured to hardships, and therefore not studious of nice accommodations. But I know not whether, for many ages, it was not considered as a part of military policy, to keep the country not easily accessible. The rocks are natural fortifications,

tions, and an enemy climbing with difficulty, was easily destroyed by those who stood high above him.

Our reception exceeded our expectations. We found nothing but civility, elegance, and plenty. After the usual refreshments, and the usual conversation, the evening came upon us. The carpet was then rolled off the floor; the musician was called, and the whole company was invited to dance, nor did ever fairies trip with greater alacrity. The general air of festivity, which predominated in this place, so far remote from all those regions which the mind has been used to contemplate as the mansions of pleasure, struck the imagination with a delightful surprise, analogous to that which is felt at an unexpected emersion from darkness into light.

When it was time to sup, the dance ceased, and six and thirty persons sat down to two tables in the same room. After supper the ladies sung *Erse* songs, to which I listened as an *English* audience to an *Italian* opera, delighted with the sounds of words which I did not understand.

I inquired the subjects of the songs, and was told of one, that it was a love song, and of another, that it was a farewell composed by one of the Islanders that was going, in this epidemical fury of emigration, to seek his fortune in *America*. What sentiments would rise, on such an occasion, in the heart of one who had not been taught to lament by precedent, I should gladly have known; but the lady, by whom I sat, thought herself not equal to the work of translating.

Mr. *Macleod* is the proprietor of the islands of *Raasay*, *Rona*, and *Fladda*, and possesses an extensive district in *Sky*. The estate has not, during four hundred years, gained

gained or loſt a ſingle acre. He acknowledges *Macleod* of Dunvegan as his chief, though his anceſtors have formerly diſputed the pre-eminence.

One of the old Highland alliances has continued for two hundred years, and is ſtill ſubſiſting between *Macleod* of *Raaſay* and *Macdonald* of *Sky*, in conſequence of which, the ſurvivor always inherits the arms of the deceaſed; a natural memorial of military friendſhip. At the death of the late Sir *James Macdonald*, his ſword was delivered to the preſent laird of *Raaſay*.

The family of *Raaſay* conſiſts of the laird, the lady, three ſons, and ten daughters. For the ſons there is a tutor in the houſe, and the lady is ſaid to be very ſkilful and diligent in the education of her girls. More gentleneſs of manners, or a more pleaſing appearance of domeſtick ſociety, is not found in the moſt poliſhed countries.

Raasay is the only inhabited island in Mr. *Macleod*'s possession. *Rona* and *Fladda* afford only pasture for cattle, of which one hundred and sixty winter in *Rona*, under the superintendence of a solitary herdsman.

The length of *Raasay* is, by computation, fifteen miles, and the breadth two. These countries have never been measured, and the computation by miles is negligent and arbitrary. We observed in travelling, that the nominal and real distance of places had very little relation to each other. *Raasay* probably contains near a hundred square miles. It affords not much ground, notwithstanding its extent, either for tillage, or pasture; for it is rough, rocky, and barren. The cattle often perish by falling from the precipices. It is like the other islands, I think, generally naked of shade, but it is naked by neglect; for the laird has an orchard, and very large forest trees grow about his house. Like other hilly countries

countries it has many rivulets. One of the brooks turns a corn-mill, and at leaft one produces trouts.

In the ftreams or frefh lakes of the iflands, I have never heard of any other fifh than trouts and eels. The trouts, which I have feen, are not large; the colour of their flefh is tinged as in *England*. Of their eels I can give no account, having never tafted them; for I believe they are not confidered as wholefome food.

It is not very eafy to fix the principles upon which mankind have agreed to eat fome animals, and reject others; and as the principle is not evident, it is not uniform. That which is felected as delicate in one country, is by its neighbours abhorred as loathfome. The Neapolitans lately refufed to eat potatoes in a famine. An Englifhman is not eafily perfuaded to dine on fnails with an Italian, on frogs with a Frenchman,

Frenchman, or on horse-flesh with a Tartar. The vulgar inhabitants of *Sky*, I know not whether of the other islands, have not only eels, but pork and bacon in abhorrence, and accordingly I never saw a hog in the *Hebrides*, except one at *Dunvegan*.

Raasay has wild fowl in abundance, but neither deer, hares, nor rabbits. Why it has them not, might be asked, but that of such questions there is no end. Why does any nation want what it might have? Why are not spices transplanted to *America*? Why does tea continue to be brought from China? Life improves but by slow degrees, and much in every place is yet to do. Attempts have been made to raise roebucks in *Raasay*, but without effect. The young ones it is extremely difficult to rear, and the old can very seldom be taken alive.

Hares

Hares and rabbits might be more eafily obtained. That they have few or none of either in *Sky*, they impute to the ravage of the foxes, and have therefore fet, for fome years paft, a price upon their heads, which, as the number was diminifhed, has been gradually raifed, from three fhillings and fixpence to a guinea, a fum fo great in this part of the world, that, in a fhort time, *Sky* may be as free from foxes, as *England* from wolves. The fund for thefe rewards is a tax of fixpence in the pound, impofed by the farmers on themfelves, and faid to be paid with great willingnefs.

The beafts of prey in the Iflands are foxes, otters, and weafels. The foxes are bigger than thofe of *England*; but the otters exceed ours in a far greater proportion. I faw one at *Armidel*, of a fize much beyond that which I fuppofed them ever to attain; and Mr. *Maclean*, the heir

of

of *Col*, a man of middle stature, informed me that he once shot an otter, of which the tail reached the ground, when he held up the head to a level with his own. I expected the otter to have a foot particularly formed for the art of swimming; but upon examination, I did not find it differing much from that of a spaniel. As he preys in the sea, he does little visible mischief, and is killed only for his fur. White otters are sometimes seen.

In *Raasay* they might have hares and rabbits, for they have no foxes. Some depredations, such as were never made before, have caused a suspicion that a fox has been lately landed in the island by spite or wantonness. This imaginary stranger has never yet been seen, and therefore, perhaps, the mischief was done by some other animal. It is not likely that a creature so ungentle, whose head could have been sold in *Sky* for a guinea, should be kept alive only

only to gratify the malice of sending him to prey upon a neighbour: and the passage from *Sky* is wider than a fox would venture to swim, unless he were chased by dogs into the sea, and perhaps then his strength would enable him to cross. How beasts of prey came into any islands is not easy to guess. In cold countries they take advantage of hard winters, and travel over the ice: but this is a very scanty solution; for they are found where they have no discoverable means of coming.

The corn of this island is but little. I saw the harvest of a small field. The women reaped the corn, and the men bound up the sheaves. The strokes of the sickle were timed by the modulation of the harvest song, in which all their voices were united. They accompany in the Highlands every action, which can be done in equal time, with an appropriated strain, which has, they say, not much meaning; but

its

its effects are regularity and cheerfulness. The ancient proceleusmatick song, by which the rowers of gallies were animated, may be supposed to have been of this kind. There is now an *oar-song* used by the *Hebridians.*

The ground of *Raasay* seems fitter for cattle than for corn, and of black cattle I suppose the number is very great. The Laird himself keeps a herd of four hundred, one hundred of which are annually sold. Of an extensive domain, which he holds in his own hands, he considers the sale of cattle as repaying him the rent, and supports the plenty of a very liberal table with the remaining product.

Raasay is supposed to have been very long inhabited. On one side of it they show caves, into which the rude nations of the first ages retreated from the weather. These dreary vaults might have had other uses.
There

There is still a cavity near the house called the *oar-cave*, in which the seamen, after one of those piratical expeditions, which in rougher times was very frequent, used, as tradition tells, to hide their oars. This hollow was near the sea, that nothing so necessary might be far to be fetched; and it was secret, that enemies, if they landed, could find nothing. Yet it is not very evident of what use it was to hide their oars from those, who, if they were masters of the coast, could take away their boats.

A proof much stronger of the distance at which the first possessors of this island lived from the present time, is afforded by the stone heads of arrows which are very frequently picked up. The people call them *Elf-bolts*, and believe that the fairies shoot them at the cattle. They nearly resemble those which Mr. *Banks* has lately brought from the savage countries in the Pacifick Ocean, and

and muſt have been made by a nation to which the uſe of metals was unknown.

The number of this little community has never been counted by its ruler, nor have I obtained any poſitive account, conſiſtent with the reſult of political computation. Not many years ago, the late Laird led out one hundred men upon a military expedition. The ſixth part of a people is ſuppoſed capable of bearing arms: *Raaſay* had therefore ſix hundred inhabitants. But becauſe it is not likely, that every man able to ſerve in the field would follow the ſummons, or that the chief would leave his lands totally defenceleſs, or take away all the hands qualified for labour, let it be ſuppoſed, that half as many might be permitted to ſtay at home. The whole number will then be nine hundred, or nine to a ſquare mile; a degree of populouſneſs greater than thoſe tracts of deſolation can often

often show. They are content with their country, and faithful to their chiefs, and yet uninfected with the fever of migration.

Near the house at *Raasay*, is a chapel unroofed and ruinous, which has long been used only as a place of burial. About the churches, in the islands, are small squares inclosed with stone, which belong to particular families, as repositories for the dead. At *Raasay* there is one, I think, for the proprietor, and one for some collateral house.

It is told by *Martin*, that at the death of the Lady of the Island, it has been here the custom to erect a cross. This we found not to be true. The stones that stand about the chapel at a small distance, some of which perhaps have crosses cut upon them, are believed to have been not funeral monuments, but the ancient boundaries of the sanctuary or consecrated ground.

Martin

Martin was a man not illiterate: he was an inhabitant of *Sky*, and therefore was within reach of intelligence, and with no great difficulty might have visited the places which he undertakes to describe; yet with all his opportunities, he has often suffered himself to be deceived. He lived in the last century, when the chiefs of the clans had lost little of their original influence. The mountains were yet unpenetrated, no inlet was opened to foreign novelties, and the feudal institutions operated upon life with their full force. He might therefore have displayed a series of subordination and a form of government, which, in more luminous and improved regions, have been long forgotten, and have delighted his readers with many uncouth customs that are now disused, and wild opinions that prevail no longer. But he probably had not knowledge of the world sufficient to qualify him for judging what would deserve or gain the attention of mankind.

The

The mode of life which was familiar to himſelf, he did not ſuppoſe unknown to others, nor imagined that he could give pleaſure by telling that of which it was, in his little country, impoſſible to be ignorant.

What he has neglected cannot now be performed. In nations, where there is hardly the uſe of letters, what is once out of ſight is loſt for ever. They think but little, and of their few thoughts, none are waſted on the paſt, in which they are neither intereſted by fear nor hope. Their only regiſters are ſtated obſervances and practical repreſentations. For this reaſon an age of ignorance is an age of ceremony. Pageants, and proceſſions, and commemorations, gradually ſhrink away, as better methods come into uſe of recording events, and preſerving rights.

It is not only in *Raaſay* that the chapel is unroofed and uſeleſs; through the few islands which we visited, we neither saw nor heard of any house of prayer, except in *Sky*, that was not in ruins. The malignant influence of *Calvinism* has blasted ceremony and decency together; and if the remembrance of papal superstition is obliterated, the monuments of papal piety are likewise effaced.

It has been, for many years, popular to talk of the lazy devotion of the Romish clergy; over the sleepy laziness of men that erected churches, we may indulge our superiority with a new triumph, by comparing it with the fervid activity of those who suffer them to fall.

Of the destruction of churches, the decay of religion must in time be the consequence; for while the public acts of the ministry are now performed in houses, a very small number can be present; and as the greater part of the Islanders make no use

of

of books, all muſt neceſſarily live in total ignorance who want the opportunity of vocal inſtruction.

From theſe remains of ancient ſanctity, which are every where to be found, it has been conjectured, that, for the laſt two centuries, the inhabitants of the Iſlands have decreaſed in number. This argument, which ſuppoſes that the churches have been ſuffered to fall, only becauſe they were no longer neceſſary, would have ſome force, if the houſes of worſhip ſtill remaining were ſufficient for the people. But ſince they have now no churches at all, theſe venerable fragments do not prove the people of former times to have been more numerous, but to have been more devout. If the inhabitants were doubled with their preſent principles, it appears not that any proviſion for publick worſhip would be made. Where the religion of a country enforces conſecrated buildings, the number of those buildings may be supposed to afford some indication, however uncertain, of the populousness of the place; but where by a change of manners a nation is contented to live without them, their decay implies no diminution of inhabitants.

Some of these dilapidations are said to be found in islands now uninhabited; but I doubt whether we can thence infer that they were ever peopled. The religion of the middle age is well known to have placed too much hope in lonely austerities. Voluntary solitude was the great art of propitiation, by which crimes were effaced, and conscience was appeased; it is therefore not unlikely, that oratories were often built in places where retirement was sure to have no disturbance.

Raasay has little that can detain a traveller, except the Laird and his family; but their power wants no auxiliaries. Such

Such a feat of hofpitality, amidft the winds and waters, fills the imagination with a delightful contrariety of images. Without is the rough ocean and the rocky land, the beating billows and the howling ftorm: within is plenty and elegance, beauty and gaiety, the fong and the dance. In *Raafay*, if I could have found an Ulyffes, I had fancied a *Phæacia*.

DUNVEGAN.

At *Raafay*, by good fortune, *Macleod*, fo the chief of the clan is called, was paying a vifit, and by him we were invited to his feat at *Dunvegan*. *Raafay* has a ftout boat, built in *Norway*, in which, with fix oars, he conveyed us back to *Sky*. We landed at *Port Re*, fo called, becaufe *James* the Fifth of *Scotland*, who had curiofity to vifit the Iflands, came into it. The port is made by an inlet of the fea, deep and narrow, where a ship lay waiting to difpeople *Sky*, by carrying the natives away to *America*.

In coafting *Sky*, we paffed by the cavern in which it was the cuftom, as *Martin* relates, to catch birds in the night, by making a fire at the entrance. This practice is difufed; for the birds, as is known often to happen, have changed their haunts.

Here we dined at a publick houfe, I believe the only inn of the ifland, and having mounted our horfes, travelled in the manner already defcribed, till we came to *Kingfborough*, a place diftinguifhed by that name, becaufe the King lodged here when he landed at *Port Re*. We were entertained with the ufual hofpitality by Mr. *Macdonald* and his lady *Flora Macdonald*, a name that will be mentioned in hiftory, and if courage and fidelity be virtues, mentioned with honour. She is a woman of middle ftature,

foft

soft features, gentle manners, and elegant presence.

In the morning we sent our horses round a promontory to meet us, and spared ourselves part of the day's fatigue, by crossing an arm of the sea. We had at last some difficulty in coming to *Dunvegan*; for our way led over an extensive moor, where every step was to be taken with caution, and we were often obliged to alight, because the ground could not be trusted. In travelling this watery flat, I perceived that it had a visible declivity, and might without much expence or difficulty be drained. But difficulty and expence are relative terms, which have different meanings in different places.

To *Dunvegan* we came, very willing to be at rest, and found our fatigue amply recompensed by our reception. Lady *Macleod*, who had lived many years in *England*, was newly come hither with her son and four daughters, who knew all the arts of southern elegance, and all the modes of English economy. Here therefore we settled, and did not spoil the present hour with thoughts of departure.

Dunvegan is a rocky prominence, that juts out into a bay, on the west side of *Sky*. The house, which is the principal seat of *Macleod*, is partly old and partly modern; it is built upon the rock, and looks upon the water. It forms two sides of a small square: on the third side is the skeleton of a castle of unknown antiquity, supposed to have been a *Norwegian* fortress, when the Danes were masters of the Islands. It is so nearly entire, that it might have easily been made habitable, were there not an ominous tradition in the family, that the owner shall not long outlive the reparation. The grandfather of the present Laird, in defiance of prediction, began the work, but desisted

desisted in a little time, and applied his money to worse uses.

As the inhabitants of the *Hebrides* lived, for many ages, in continual expectation of hostilities, the chief of every clan resided in a fortress. This house was accessible only from the water, till the last possessor opened an entrance by stairs upon the land.

They had formerly reason to be afraid, not only of declared wars and authorized invaders, or of roving pirates, which, in the northern seas, must have been very common; but of inroads and insults from rival clans, who, in the plenitude of feudal independence, asked no leave of their Sovereign to make war on one another. *Sky* has been ravaged by a feud between the two mighty powers of *Macdonald* and *Macleod*. *Macdonald* having married a *Macleod*, upon some discontent dismissed her, perhaps because she had brought him no children.

Before

Before the reign of *James* the Fifth, a Highland Laird made a trial of his wife for a certain time, and if she did not please him, he was then at liberty to send her away. This however must always have offended, and *Macleod* resenting the injury, whatever were its circumstances, declared, that the wedding had been solemnized without a bonfire, but that the separation should be better illuminated; and raising a little army, set fire to the territories of *Macdonald*, who returned the visit, and prevailed.

Another story may show the disorderly state of insular neighbourhood. The inhabitants of the Isle of *Egg*, meeting a boat manned by *Macleods*, tied the crew hand and foot, and set them a-drift. *Macleod* landed upon *Egg*, and demanded the offenders; but the inhabitants refusing to surrender them, retreated to a cavern, into which they thought their enemies unlikely to follow them. *Macleod* choked them with

with smoke, and left them lying dead by families as they stood.

Here the violence of the weather confined us for some time, not at all to our discontent or inconvenience. We would indeed very willingly have visited the Islands, which might be seen from the house scattered in the sea, and I was particularly desirous to have viewed *Isay*; but the storms did not permit us to launch a boat, and we were condemned to listen in idleness to the wind, except when we were better engaged by listening to the ladies.

We had here more winds than waves, and suffered the severity of a tempest, without enjoying its magnificence. The sea being broken by the multitude of islands, does not roar with so much noise, nor beat the storm with such foamy violence, as I have remarked on the coast of *Sussex*. Though, while I was in the *Hebrides*, the
wind

wind was extremely turbulent, I never saw very high billows.

The country about *Dunvegan* is rough and barren. There are no trees, except in the orchard, which is a low sheltered spot surrounded with a wall.

When this house was intended to sustain a siege, a well was made in the court, by boring the rock downwards, till water was found, which though so near to the sea, I have not heard mentioned as brackish, though it has some hardness, or other qualities, which makes it less fit for use; and the family is now better supplied from a stream, which runs by the rock, from two pleasing water-falls.

Here we saw some traces of former manners, and heard some standing traditions. In the house is kept an ox's horn, hollowed so as to hold perhaps two quarts,

which

which the heir of *Macleod* was expected to swallow at one draught, as a test of his manhood, before he was permitted to bear arms, or could claim a seat among the men. It is held that the return of the Laird to *Dunvegan*, after any considerable absence, produces a plentiful capture of herrings; and that, if any woman crosses the water to the opposite Island, the herrings will desert the coast. *Boetius* tells the same of some other place. This tradition is not uniform. Some hold that no woman may pass, and others that none may pass but a *Macleod*.

Among other guests, which the hospitality of *Dunvegan* brought to the table, a visit was paid by the Laird and Lady of a small island south of *Sky*, of which the proper name is *Muack*, which signifies swine. It is commonly called *Muck*, which the proprietor not liking, has endeavoured, without effect, to change to *Monk*. It is usual to call gentlemen in *Scotland* by the name of their possessions,

possessions, as *Raasay*, *Bernera*, *Loch Buy*, a practice necessary in countries inhabited by clans, where all that live in the same territory have one name, and must be therefore discriminated by some addition. This gentleman, whose name, I think, is *Maclean*, should be regularly called *Muck*; but the appellation, which he thinks too coarse for his Island, he would like still less for himself, and he is therefore addressed by the title of, *Isle of Muck*.

This little island, however it be named, is of considerable value. It is too *English* miles long, and three quarters of a mile broad, and consequently contains only nine hundred and sixty *English* acres. It is chiefly arable. Half of this little dominion the Laird retains in his own hand, and on the other half, live one hundred and sixty persons, who pay their rent by exported corn. What rent they pay, we were not told, and could not decently inquire.

quire. The proportion of the people to the land is such, as the most fertile countries do not commonly maintain.

The Laird having all his people under his immediate view, seems to be very attentive to their happiness. The devastation of the small-pox, when it visits places where it comes seldom, is well known. He has disarmed it of its terrour at *Muack*, by inoculating eighty of his people. The expence was two shillings and sixpence a head. Many trades they cannot have among them, but upon occasion, he fetches a smith from the Isle of *Egg*, and has a tailor from the main land, six times a year. This Island well deserved to be seen, but the Laird's absence left us no opportunity.

Every inhabited Island has its appendant and subordinate islets. *Muck*, however small, has yet others smaller about it, one of which has only ground sufficient to afford pasture for three wethers.

At *Dungevan* I had tasted lotus, and was in danger of forgetting that I was ever to depart, till Mr. Boswell sagely reproached me with my sluggishness and softness. I had no very forcible defence to make; and we agreed to pursue our journey. *Macleod* accompanied us to *Ulinish*, where we were entertained by the sheriff of the Island.

ULINISH.

Mr. *Macqueen* travelled with us, and directed our attention to all that was worthy of observation. With him we went to see an ancient building, called a dun or borough. It was a circular inclosure, about forty-two feet in diameter, walled round with loose stones, perhaps to the height of nine feet. The walls are very thick, diminishing a little towards the top, and though in these countries, stone is not brought far, must have been raised with much labour. Within the great circle were several

several smaller rounds of wall, which formed distinct apartments. Its date and its use are unknown. Some suppose it the original seat of the chiefs of the *Macleods*. Mr. *Macqueen* thought it a *Danish* fort.

The entrance is covered with flat stones, and is narrow, because it was necessary that the stones which lie over it, should reach from one wall to the other; yet, strait as the passage is, they seem heavier than could have been placed where they now lie, by the naked strength of as many men as might stand about them. They were probably raised by putting long pieces of wood under them, to which the action of a long line of lifters might be applied. Savages, in all countries, have patience proportionate to their unskilfulness, and are content to attain their end by very tedious methods.

If it was ever roofed, it might once have been a dwelling, but as there is no provision for water, it could not have been a fortress. In *Sky*, as in every other place, there is an ambition of exalting whatever has survived memory, to some important use, and referring it to very remote ages. I am inclined to suspect, that in lawless times, when the inhabitants of every mountain stole the cattle of their neighbour, these enclosures were used to secure the herds and flocks in the night. When they were driven within the wall, they might be easily watched, and defended as long as could be needful; for the robbers durst not wait till the injured clan should find them in the morning.

The interior enclosures, if the whole building were once a house, were the chambers of the chief inhabitants. If it was a place of security for cattle, they were probably the shelters of the keepers.

From the *Dun* we were conducted to another place of security, a cave carried a
great

great way under ground, which had been discovered by digging after a fox. These caves, of which many have been found, and many probably remain concealed, are formed, I believe, commonly by taking advantage of a hollow, where banks or rocks rise on either side. If no such place can be found, the ground must be cut away. The walls are made by piling stones against the earth, on either side. It is then roofed by large stones laid across the cavern, which therefore cannot be wide. Over the roof, turfs were placed, and grass was suffered to grow; and the mouth was concealed by bushes, or some other cover.

These caves were represented to us as the cabins of the first rude inhabitants, of which, however, I am by no means persuaded. This was so low, that no man could stand upright in it. By their construction they are all so narrow, that two can never pass along them together, and being subterraneous, they must be always damp. They are not the work of an age much ruder than the present; for they are formed with as much art as the construction of a common hut requires. I imagine them to have been places only of occasional use, in which the Islander, upon a sudden alarm, hid his utensils, or his clothes, and perhaps sometimes his wife and children.

This cave we entered, but could not proceed the whole length, and went away without knowing how far it was carried. For this omission we shall be blamed, as we perhaps have blamed other travellers; but the day was rainy, and the ground was damp. We had with us neither spades nor pickaxes, and if love of ease surmounted our desire of knowledge, the offence has not the invidiousness of singularity.

Edifices, either standing or ruined, are the chief records of an illiterate nation. In some

some part of this journey, at no great distance from our way, stood a shattered fortress, of which the learned minister, to whose communication we are much indebted, gave us an account.

Those, said he, are the walls of a place of refuge, built in the time of James the Sixth, by Hugh Macdonald, who was next heir to the dignity and fortune of his chief. Hugh, being so near his wish, was impatient of delay; and had art and influence sufficient to engage several gentlemen in a plot against the Laird's life. Something must be stipulated on both sides; for they would not dip their hands in blood merely for Hugh's advancement. The compact was formally written, signed by the conspirators, and placed in the hands of one Macleod.

It happened that Macleod had sold some cattle to a drover, who not having ready money,

money, gave him a bond for payment. The debt was discharged, and the bond redemanded; which Macleod, who could not read, intending to put into his hands, gave him the conspiracy. The drover, when he had read the paper, delivered it privately to Macdonald, who being thus informed of his danger, called his friends together, and provided for his safety. He made a public feast, and inviting Hugh Macdonald and his confederates, placed each of them at the table between two men of known fidelity. The compact of conspiracy was then shewn, and every man confronted with his own name. Macdonald acted with great moderation. He upbraided Hugh, both with disloyalty and ingratitude; but told the rest, that he considered them as men deluded and misinformed. Hugh was sworn to fidelity, and dismissed with his companions; but he was not generous enough to be reclaimed by lenity; and finding no longer any countenance

nance among the gentlemen, endeavoured to execute the fame defign by meaner hands. In this practice he was detected, taken to Macdonald's caftle, and imprifoned in the dungeon. When he was hungry, they let down a plentiful meal of falted meat; and when, after his repaft, he called for drink, conveyed to him a covered cup, which, when he lifted the lid, he found empty. From that time they vifited him no more, but left him to perifh in folitude and darknefs.

We were then told of a cavern by the fea-fide, remarkable for the powerful reverberation of founds. After dinner, we took a boat, to explore this curious cavity. The boatmen, who feemed to be of a rank above that of common drudges, inquired who the ftrangers were, and being told we came one from *Scotland*, and the other from *England*, afked if the *Englifhman* could recount a long genealogy. What answer was given them, the conversation being in *Erse*, I was not much inclined to examine.

They expected no good event of the voyage; for one of them declared that he heard the cry of an *English* ghost. This omen I was not told till after our return, and therefore cannot claim the dignity of despising it.

The sea was smooth. We never left the shore, and came without any disaster to the cavern, which we found rugged and misshapen, about one hundred and eighty feet long, thirty wide in the broadest part, and in the loftiest, as we guessed, about thirty high. It was now dry, but at high water the sea rises in it near six feet. Here I saw what I had never seen before, limpets and muscles in their natural state. But, as a new testimony to the veracity of

common

common fame, here was no echo to be heard.

We then walked through a natural arch in the rock, which might have pleased us by its novelty, had the stones, which encumbered our feet, given us leisure to consider it. We were shown the gummy seed of the kelp, that fastens itself to a stone, from which it grows into a strong stalk.

In our return, we found a little boy upon the point of a rock, catching with his angle, a supper for the family. We rowed up to him, and borrowed his rod, with which Mr. *Boswell* caught a cuddy.

The cuddy is a fish of which I know not the philosophical name. It is not much bigger than a gudgeon, but is of great use in these Islands, as it affords the lower people both food, and oil for their lamps. Cuddies are so abundant, at some times of

the

the year, that they are caught like white-bait in the Thames, only by dipping a basket and drawing it back.

If it were always practicable to fish, these Islands could never be in much danger from famine; but unhappily in the winter, when other provision fails, the seas are commonly too rough for nets, or boats.

TALISKER IN SKY.

From *Ulinish*, our next stage was to *Talisker*, the house of Colonel *Macleod*, an officer in the *Dutch* service, who in this time of universal peace, has for several years been permitted to be absent from his regiment. Having been bred to physick, he is consequently a scholar, and his lady, by accompanying him in his different places of residence, is become skilful in several languages. *Talisker* is the place beyond all that I have seen, from which the gay and the jovial seem utterly excluded; and where the hermit might expect to grow old in meditation, without possibility of disturbance or interruption. It is situated very near the sea, but upon a coast where no vessel lands but when it is driven by a tempest on the rocks. Towards the land are lofty hills streaming with water-falls. The garden is sheltered by firs, or pines, which grow there so prosperously, that some, which the present inhabitant planted, are very high and thick.

At this place we very happily met Mr. *Donald Maclean*, a young gentleman, the eldest son of the Laird of *Col*, heir to a very great extent of land, and so desirous of improving his inheritance, that he spent a considerable time among the farmers of *Hertfordshire*, and *Hampshire*, to learn their practice. He worked with his own hands at the principal operations of agriculture, that he might not deceive himself

by

by a false opinion of skill, which if he should find it deficient at home, he had no means of completing. If the world has agreed to praise the travels and manual labours to the Czar of *Muscovy*, let *Col* have his share of the like applause, in the proportion of his dominions to the empire of *Russia*.

This young gentleman was sporting in the mountains of *Sky*, and when he was weary with following his game, repaired for lodging to *Talisker*. At night he missed one of his dogs, and when he went to seek him in the morning, found two eagles feeding on his carcass.

Col, for he must be named by his possessions, hearing that our intention was to visit *Jona*, offered to conduct us to his chief, Sir *Allan Maclean*, who lived in the isle of *Inch Kenneth*, and would readily find us a convenient passage. From this time

time was formed an acquaintance, which being begun by kindnefs, was accidentally continued by conftraint; we derived much pleafure from it, and I hope have given him no reafon to repent it.

The weather was now almoft one continued ftorm, and we were to fnatch fome happy intermiffion to be conveyed to *Mull*, the third Ifland of the *Hebrides*, lying about a degree fouth of *Sky*, whence we might eafily find our way to *Inch Kenneth*, where Sir *Allan Maclean* refided, and afterward to *Jona*.

For this purpofe, the moft commodious ftation that we could take was *Armidel*, which Sir *Alexander Macdonald* had now left to a gentleman, who lived there as his factor or fteward.

In our way to *Armidel*, was Coriatachan, where we had already been, and to which therefore we were very willing to return.

We

We ſtaid however ſo long at *Taliſker*, that a great part of our journey was performed in the gloom of the evening. In travelling even thus almoſt without light thro' naked ſolitude, when there is a guide whoſe conduct may be truſted, a mind not naturally too much diſpoſed to fear, may preſerve ſome degree of cheerfulneſs; but what muſt be the ſolicitude of him who ſhould be wandering, among the craggs and hollows, benighted, ignorant, and alone?

The fictions of the *Gothick* romances were not ſo remote from credibility as they are now thought. In the full prevalence of the feudal inſtitution, when violence deſolated the world, and every baron lived in a fortreſs, foreſts and caſtles were regularly ſucceeded by each other, and the adventurer might very ſuddenly paſs from the gloom of woods, or the ruggedneſs of moors, to ſeats of plenty, gaiety, and magnificence. Whatever is imaged in the wildeſt tale,

tale, if giants, dragons, and enchantment be excepted, would be felt by him, who, wandering in the mountains without a guide, or upon the sea without a pilot, should be carried amidst his terrour and uncertainty, to the hospitality and elegance of *Raasay* and *Dunvegan*.

To Coriatachan at last we came, and found ourselves welcomed as before. Here we staid two days, and made such inquiries as curiosity suggested. The house was filled with company, among whom Mr. *Macpherson* and his sister distinguished themselves by their politeness and accomplishments. By him we were invited to *Ostig*, a house not far from *Armidel*, where we might easily hear of a boat, when the weather would suffer us to leave the Island.

OSTIG IN SKY.

At *Ostig*, of which Mr. *Macpherson* is minister, we were entertained for some days,
then

then removed to *Armidel*, where we finished our observations on the island of Sky.

As this island lies in the fifty-seventh degree, the air cannot be supposed to have much warmth. The long continuance of the sun above the horizon, does indeed sometimes produce great heat in northern latitudes; but this can only happen in sheltered places, where the atmosphere is to a certain degree stagnant, and the same mass of air continues to receive for many hours the rays of the sun, and the vapours of the earth. *Sky* lies open on the west and north to a vast extent of ocean, and is cooled in the summer by a perpetual ventilation, but by the same blasts is kept warm in winter. Their weather is not pleasing. Half the year is deluged with rain. From the autumnal to the vernal equinox, a dry day is hardly known, except when the showers are suspended by a tempest. Under such skies can be expected no great exuberance

berance of vegetation. Their winter overtakes their summer, and their harvest lies upon the ground drenched with rain. The autumn struggles hard to produce some of our early fruits. I gathered gooseberries in September; but they were small, and the husk was thick.

Their winter is seldom such as puts a full stop to the growth of plants, or reduces the cattle to live wholly on the surplusage of the summer. In the year Seventy-one they had a severe season, remembered by the name of the Black Spring, from which the island has not yet recovered. The snow lay long upon the ground, a calamity hardly known before. Part of their cattle died for want, part were unseasonably sold to buy sustenance for the owners; and, what I have not read or heard of before, the kine that survived were so emaciated and dispirited, that they did not require
the

the male at the usual time. Many of the roebucks perished.

The soil, as in other countries, has its diversities. In some parts there is only a thin layer of earth spread upon a rock, which bears nothing but short brown heath, and perhaps is not generally capable of any better product. There are many bogs or mosses of greater or less extent, where the soil cannot be supposed to want depth, though it is too wet for the plough. But we did not observe in these any aquatick plants. The vallies and the mountains are alike darkened with heath. Some grass, however, grows here and there, and some happier spots of earth are capable of tillage.

Their agriculture is laborious, and perhaps rather feeble than unskilful. Their chief manure is sea-weed, which, when they lay it to rot upon the field, gives them a better crop than those of the Highlands. They

heap

heap sea-shells upon the dunghill, which in time moulder into a fertilising substance. When they find a vein of earth where they cannot use it, they dig it up, and add it to the mould of a more commodious place.

Their corn grounds often lie in such intricacies among the craggs, that there is no room for the action of a team and plough. The soil is then turned up by manual labour with an instrument called a crooked spade, of a form and weight which to me appeared very incommodious, and would perhaps be soon improved in a country where workmen could be easily found and easily paid. It has a narrow blade of iron fixed to a long and heavy piece of wood, which must have, about a foot and a half above the iron, a knee or flexure with the angle downwards. When the farmer encounters a stone which is the great impediment of his operations, he drives the blade under it, and bringing the knee or angle to the ground, has in the long handle a very forcible lever.

According to the different mode of tillage, farms are diftinguifhed into *long land* and *fhort land*. Long land is that which affords room for a plough, and fhort land is turned up by the fpade.

The grain which they commit to the furrows thus tedioufly formed, is either oats or barley. They do not fow barley without very copious manure, and then they expect from it ten for one, an increafe equal to that of better countries; but the culture is fo operofe that they content themfelves commonly with oats; and who can relate without compaffion, that after all their diligence they are to expect only a triple increafe? It is in vain to hope for plenty, when a third part of the harveft muft be referved for feed.

When their grain is arrived at the state which they must consider as ripeness, they do not cut, but pull the barley: to the oats they apply the sickle. Wheel carriages they have none, but make a frame of timber, which is drawn by one horse with the two points behind pressing on the ground. On this they sometimes drag home their sheaves, but often convey them home in a kind of open panier, or frame of sticks upon the horse's back.

Of that which is obtained with so much difficulty, nothing surely ought to be wasted; yet their method of clearing their oats from the husk is by parching them in the straw. Thus with the genuine improvidence of savages, they destroy that fodder for want of which their cattle may perish. From this practice they have two petty conveniencies. They dry the grain so that it is easily reduced to meal, and they escape the theft of the thresher. The taste contracted from the fire by the oats, as by every other scorched substance, use must long ago have made grateful. The oats that are not parched must be dried in a kiln.

The barns of *Sky* I never saw. That which *Macleod* of *Raasay* had erected near his house was so contrived, because the harvest is seldom brought home dry, as by perpetual perflation to prevent the mow from heating.

Of their gardens I can judge only from their tables. I did not observe that the common greens were wanting, and suppose, that by choosing an advantageous exposition, they can raise all the more hardy esculent plants. Of vegetable fragrance or beauty they are not yet studious. Few vows are made to Flora in the *Hebrides*.

They gather a little hay, but the grass is mown late; and is so often almost dry and again

again very wet, before it is housed, that it becomes a collection of withered stalks without taste or fragrance; it must be eaten by cattle that have nothing else, but by most English farmers would be thrown away.

In the Islands I have not heard that any subterraneous treasures have been discovered, though where there are mountains, there are commonly minerals. One of the rocks in *Col* has a black vein, imagined to consist of the ore of lead; but it was never yet opened or essayed. In *Sky* a black mass was accidentally picked up, and brought into the house of the owner of the land, who found himself strongly inclined to think it a coal, but unhappily it did not burn in the chimney. Common ores would be here of no great value; for what requires to be separated by fire, must, if it were found, be carried away in its mineral state, here being no fewel for the smelting house or forge. Perhaps by diligent search in this world of stone, some valuable species of marble might be discovered. But neither philosophical curiosity, nor commercial industry, have yet fixed their abode here, where the importunity of immediate want supplied but for the day, and craving on the morrow, has left little room for excursive knowledge or the pleasing fancies of distant profit.

They have lately found a manufacture considerably lucrative. Their rocks abound with kelp, a sea-plant, of which the ashes are melted into glass. They burn kelp in great quantities, and then send it away in ships, which come regularly to purchase them. This new source of riches has raised the rents of many maritime farms; but the tenants pay, like all other tenants, the additional rent with great unwillingness; because they consider the profits of the kelp as the mere product of personal labour, to which the landlord contributes nothing.

How-

However, as any man may be said to give what he gives the power of gaining, he has certainly as much right to profit from the price of kelp as of any thing else found or raised upon his ground.

This new trade has excited a long and eager litigation between *Macdonald* and *Macleod*, for a ledge of rocks, which, till the value of kelp was known, neither of them desired the reputation of possessing.

The cattle of *Sky* are not so small as is commonly believed. Since they have sent their beeves in great numbers to southern marts, they have probably taken more care of their breed. At stated times the annual growth of cattle is driven to a fair, by a general drover, and with the money, which he returns to the farmer, the rents are paid.

The price regularly expected, is from two to three pounds a head: there was once
one

one sold for five pounds. They go from the Islands very lean, and are not offered to the butcher, till they have been long fatted in *English* pastures.

Of their black cattle, some are without horns, called by the Scots *humble* cows, as we call a bee an *humble* bee, that wants a sting. Whether this difference be specifick, or accidental, though we inquired with great diligence, we could not be informed. We are not very sure that the bull is ever without horns, though we have been told, that such bulls there are. What is produced by putting a horned and unhorned male and female together, no man has ever tried, that thought the result worthy of observation.

Their horses are, like their cows, of a moderate size. I had no difficulty to mount myself commodiously by the favour of the gentlemen. I heard of very little cows in *Barra*, and very little horses in *Rum*, where perhaps no care is taken to prevent that diminution of fize, which muſt always happen, where the greater and the leſs copulate promiſcuouſly, and the young animal is reſtrained from growth by penury of fuſtenance.

The goat is the general inhabitant of the earth, complying with every difference of climate, and of foil. The goats of the *Hebrides* are like others: nor did I hear any thing of their ſheep, to be particularly remarked.

In the penury of theſe malignant regions nothing is left that can be converted to food. The goats and the ſheep are milked like the cows. A fingle meal of a goat is a quart, and of a ſheep a pint. Such at leaſt was the account, which I could extract from thoſe of whom I am not fure that they ever had inquired.

The

The milk of goats is much thinner than that of cows, and that of sheep is much thicker. Sheeps milk is never eaten before it is boiled: as it is thick, it must be very liberal of curd, and the people of *St. Kilda* form it into small cheeses.

The stags of the mountains are less than those of our parks, or forests, perhaps not bigger than our fallow deer. Their flesh has no rankness, nor is inferiour in flavour to our common venison. The roebuck I neither saw nor tasted. These are not countries for a regular chase. The deer are not driven with horns and hounds. A sportsman, with his gun in his hand, watches the animal, and when he has wounded him, traces him by the blood.

They have a race of brinded greyhounds larger and stronger than those with which we course hares, and those are the only dogs used by them for the chase.

Man

Man is by the use of fire-arms made so much an overmatch for other animals, that in all countries, where they are in use, the wild part of the creation sensibly diminishes. There will probably not be long either stags or roebucks in the Islands. All the beasts of chase would have been lost long ago in countries well inhabited, had they not been preserved by laws for the pleasure of the rich.

There are in *Sky* neither rats nor mice, but the weasel is so frequent, that he is heard in houses rattling behind chests or beds, as rats in *England*. They probably owe to his predominance that they have no other vermin; for since the great rat took possession of this part of the world, scarce a ship can touch at any port, but some of his race are left behind. They have within these few years began to infest the Isle of *Col*, where being left by some trading vessel, veffel, they have increafed for want of weafels to oppofe them.

The inhabitants of *Sky*, and of the other Iflands, which I have feen, are commonly of the middle ftature, with fewer among them very tall or very fhort, than are feen in *England*, or perhaps, as their numbers are fmall, the chances of any deviation from the common meafure are neceffarily few. The talleft men that I faw are among thofe of higher rank. In regions of barrennefs and fcarcity, the human race is hindered in its growth by the fame caufes as other animals.

The ladies have as much beauty here as in other places, but bloom and foftnefs are not to be expected among the lower claffes, whofe faces are expofed to the rudenefs of the climate, and whofe features are fometimes contracted by want, and fometimes hardened by the blafts. Supreme beauty is seldom found in cottages or work-shops, even where no real hardships are suffered. To expand the human face to its full perfection, it seems necessary that the mind should co-operate by placidness of content, or consciousness of superiority.

Their strength is proportionate to their size, but they are accustomed to run upon rough ground, and therefore can with great agility skip over the bog, or clamber the mountain. For a campaign in the wastes of *America*, soldiers better qualified could not have been found. Having little work to do, they are not willing, nor perhaps able to endure a long continuance of manual labour, and are therefore considered as habitually idle.

Having never been supplied with these accommodations, which life extensively diversified with trades affords, they supply their wants by very insufficient shifts,
and

and endure many inconveniences, which a little attention would eaſily relieve. I have ſeen a horſe carrying home the harveſt on a crate. Under his tail was a ſtick for a crupper, held at the two ends by twiſts of ſtraw. Hemp will grow in their iſlands, and therefore ropes may be had. If they wanted hemp, they might make better cordage of ruſhes, or perhaps of nettles, than of ſtraw.

Their method of life neither ſecures them perpetual health, nor expoſes them to any particular diſeaſes. There are phyſicians in the Iſlands, who, I believe, all practiſe chirurgery, and all compound their own medicines.

It is generally ſuppoſed, that life is longer in places where there are few opportunities of luxury; but I found no inſtance here of extraordinary longevity. A cottager grows old over his oaten cakes, like

like a citizen at a turtle feaſt. He is indeed ſeldom incommoded by corpulence. Poverty preſerves him from ſinking under the burden of himſelf, but he eſcapes no other injury of time. Inſtances of long life are often related, which thoſe who hear them are more willing to credit than examine. To be told that any man has attained a hundred years, gives hope and comfort to him who ſtands trembling on the brink of his own climacterick.

Length of life is diſtributed impartially to very different modes of life in very different climates; and the mountains have no greater examples of age and health than the low lands, where I was introduced to two ladies of high quality; one of whom, in her ninety-fourth year, preſided at her table with the full exerciſe of all her powers; and the other has attained her eighty-fourth, without any diminution of her vivacity,

and

and with little reason to accuse time of depredations on her beauty.

In the Islands, as in most other places, the inhabitants are of different rank, and one does not encroach here upon another. Where there is no commerce nor manufacture, he that is born poor can scarce become rich; and if none are able to buy estates, he that is born to land cannot annihilate his family by selling it. This was once the state of these countries. Perhaps there is no example, till within a century and half, of any family whose estate was alienated otherwise than by violence or forfeiture. Since money has been brought amongst them, they have found, like others, the art of spending more than they receive; and I saw with grief the chief of a very ancient clan, whose Island was condemned by law to be sold for the satisfaction of his creditors.

The

The name of highest dignity is Laird, of which there are in the extensive Isle of *Sky* only three, *Macdonald, Macleod,* and *Mackinnon*. The Laird is the original owner of the land, whose natural power must be very great, where no man lives but by agriculture; and where the produce of the land is not conveyed through the labyrinths of traffick, but passes directly from the hand that gathers it to the mouth that eats it. The Laird has all those in his power that live upon his farms. Kings can, for the most part, only exalt or degrade. The Laird at pleasure can feed or starve, can give bread, or withhold it. This inherent power was yet strengthened by the kindness of consanguinity, and the reverence of patriarchal authority. The Laird was the father of the Clan, and his tenants commonly bore his name. And to these principles of original command was added, for many ages, an exclusive right of legal jurisdiction.

This multifarious and extensive obligation operated with force scarcely credible. Every duty, moral or political, was absorbed in affection and adherence to the Chief. Not many years have passed since the Clans knew no law but the Laird's will. He told them to whom they should be friends or enemies, what king they should obey, and what religion they should profess.

When the Scots first rose in arms against the succession of the house of *Hanover*, *Lovat*, the Chief of the Frasers, was in exile for a rape. The Frasers were very numerous, and very zealous against the government. A pardon was sent to *Lovat*. He came to the *English* camp, and the Clan immediately deserted to him.

Next in dignity to the Laird is the Tacksman; a large taker or lease-holder of land, of which he keeps part, as a domain

main in his own hand, and lets part to under-tenants. The Tackſman is neceſſarily a man capable of ſecuring to the Laird the whole rent, and is commonly a collateral relation. Theſe *tacks*, or ſubordinate poſſeſſions, were long conſidered as hereditary, and the occupant was diſtinguiſhed by the name of the place at which he reſided. He held a middle ſtation, by which the higheſt and the loweſt orders were connected. He paid rent and reverence to the Laird, and received them from the tenants. This tenure ſtill ſubſiſts, with its original operation, but not with the primitive ſtability. Since the iſlanders, no longer content to live, have learned the deſire of growing rich, an ancient dependent is in danger of giving way to a higher bidder, at the expence of domeſtic dignity and hereditary power. The ſtranger, whoſe money buys him preference, conſiders himſelf as paying for all that he has, and is indifferent about the Laird's honour or safety. The commodiousness of money is indeed great; but there are some advantages which money cannot buy, and which therefore no wise man will by the love of money be tempted to forego.

I have found in the hither parts of *Scotland*, men not defective in judgment or general experience, who consider the Tacksman as a useless burden of the ground, as a drone who lives upon the product of an estate, without the right of property, or the merit of labour, and who impoverishes at once the landlord and the tenant. The land, say they, is let to the Tacksman at six-pence an acre, and by him to the tenant at ten-pence. Let the owner be the immediate landlord to all the tenants; if he sets the ground at eight-pence, he will increase his revenue by a fourth part, and the tenant's burden will be diminished by a fifth.

Those

Those who pursue this train of reasoning, seem not sufficiently to inquire whither it will lead them, nor to know that it will equally shew the propriety of suppressing all wholesale trade, of shutting up the shops of every man who sells what he does not make, and of extruding all whose agency and profit intervene between the manufacturer and the consumer. They may, by stretching their understandings a little wider, comprehend, that all those who by undertaking large quantities of manufacture, and affording employment to many labourers, make themselves considered as benefactors to the publick, have only been robbing their workmen with one hand, and their customers with the other. If Crowley had sold only what he could make, and all his smiths had wrought their own iron with their own hammers, he would have lived on less, and they would have sold their work for more. The salaries of superintendents and clerks would have been partly faved, and partly fhared, and nails been fometimes cheaper by a farthing in a hundred. But then if the fmith could not have found an immediate purchafer, he muft have deferted his anvil; if there had by accident at any time been more fellers than buyers, the workmen muft have reduced their profit to nothing, by underfelling one another; and as no great ftock could have been in any hand, no fudden demand of large quantities could have been anfwered, and the builder muft have ftood ftill till the nailer could fupply him.

According to thefe fchemes, univerfal plenty is to begin and end in univerfal mifery. Hope and emulation will be utterly extinguifhed; and as all muft obey the call of immediate neceffity, nothing that requires extenfive views, or provides for diftant confequences, will ever be performed.

To the southern inhabitants of Scotland, the state of the mountains and the islands is equally unknown with that of *Borneo* or *Sumatra*: Of both they have only heard a little, and guess the rest. They are strangers to the language and the manners, to the advantages and wants of the people, whose life they would model, and whose evils they would remedy.

Nothing is less difficult than to procure one convenience by the forfeiture of another. A soldier may expedite his march by throwing away his arms. To banish the Tacksman is easy, to make a country plentiful by diminishing the people, is an expeditious mode of husbandry; but that abundance, which there is nobody to enjoy, contributes little to human happiness.

As the mind must govern the hands, so in every society the man of intelligence must direct the man of labour. If the
Tacksmen

Tackſmen be taken away, the Hebrides muſt in their preſent ſtate be given up to groſsneſs and ignorance; the tenant, for want of inſtruction, will be unſkilful, and for want of admonition will be negligent. The Laird, in theſe wide eſtates, which often conſiſt of iſlands remote from one another, cannot extend his perſonal influence to all his tenants; and the ſteward having no dignity annexed to his character, can have little authority among men taught to pay reverence only to birth, and who regard the Tackſman as their hereditary ſuperior; nor can the ſteward have equal zeal for the proſperity of an eſtate profitable only to the Laird, with the Tackſman, who has the Laird's income involved in his own.

The only gentlemen in the iſlands are the Lairds, the Tackſmen, and the Miniſters, who frequently improve their livings by becoming farmers. If the Tackſmen be be banished, who will be left to impart knowledge, or impress civility? The Laird must always be at a distance from the greater part of his lands; and if he resides at all upon them, must drag his days in solitude, having no longer either a friend or a companion; he will therefore depart to some more comfortable residence, and leave the tenants to the wisdom and mercy of a factor.

Of tenants there are different orders, as they have greater or less stock. Land is sometimes leased to a small fellowship, who live in a cluster of huts, called a Tenants Town, and are bound jointly and separately for the payment of their rent. These, I believe, employ in the care of their cattle, and the labour of tillage, a kind of tenants yet lower; who having a hut, with grass for a certain number of cows and sheep, pay their rent by a stipulated quantity of labour.

The

The condition of domestic servants, or the price of occasional labour, I do not know with certainty. I was told that the maids have sheep, and are allowed to spin for their own clothing; perhaps they have no pecuniary wages, or none but in very wealthy families. The state of life which has hitherto been purely pastoral, begins now to be a little variegated with commerce; but novelties enter by degrees, and till one mode has fully prevailed over the other, no settled notion can be formed.

Such is the system of insular subordination, which, having little variety, cannot afford much delight in the view, nor long detain the mind in contemplation. The inhabitants were for a long time perhaps not unhappy; but their content was a muddy mixture of pride and ignorance, an indifference for pleasures which they did not know, a blind veneration for their chiefs,

chiefs, and a strong conviction of their own importance.

Their pride has been crushed by the heavy hand of a vindictive conqueror, whose severities have been followed by laws, which, though they cannot be called cruel, have produced much discontent, because they operate upon the surface of life, and make every eye bear witness to subjection. To be compelled to a new dress has always been found painful.

Their chiefs being now deprived of their jurisdiction, have already lost much of their influence; and as they gradually degenerate from patriarchal rulers to rapacious landlords, they will divest themselves of the little that remains.

That dignity which they derived from an opinion of their military importance, the law, which disarmed them, has abated.

An

An old gentleman, delighting himſelf with the recollection of better days, related, that forty years ago, a Chieftain walked out attended by ten or twelve followers, with their arms rattling. That animating rabble has now ceaſed. The Chief has loſt his formidable retinue; and the Highlander walks his heath unarmed and defenceleſs, with the peaceable ſubmiſſion of a French peaſant or Engliſh cottager.

Their ignorance grows every day leſs, but their knowledge is yet of little other uſe than to ſhew them their wants. They are now in the period of education, and feel the uneaſineſs of diſcipline, without yet perceiving the benefit of inſtruction.

The laſt law, by which the Highlanders are deprived of their arms, has operated with efficacy beyond expectation. Of former ſtatutes made with the ſame deſign, the execution had been feeble, and the effect incon-

inconsiderable. Concealment was undoubtedly practised, and perhaps often with connivance. There was tenderness or partiality on one side, and obstinacy on the other. But the law, which followed the victory of Culloden, found the whole nation dejected and intimidated; informations were given without danger, and without fear, and the arms were collected with such rigour, that every house was despoiled of its defence.

To disarm part of the Highlands, could give no reasonable occasion of complaint. Every government must be allowed the power of taking away the weapon that is lifted against it. But the loyal Clans murmured, with some appearance of justice, that after having defended the King, they were forbidden for the future to defend themselves; and that the sword should be forfeited, which had been legally employed. Their case is undoubtedly hard, but in
political

political regulations, good cannot be complete, it can only be predominant.

Whether by difarming a people thus broken into feveral tribes, and thus remote from the feat of power, more good than evil has been produced, may deferve inquiry. The fupreme power in every community has the right of debarring every individual, and every fubordinate fociety, from felf-defence, only becaufe the fupreme power is able to defend them; and therefore where the governor cannot act, he muft truft the fubject to act for himfelf. Thefe Iflands might be wafted with fire and fword before their fovereign would know their diftrefs. A gang of robbers, fuch as has been lately found confederating themfelves in the Highlands, might lay a wide region under contribution. The crew of a petty privateer might land on the largeft and moft wealthy of the Iflands, and riot without control in cruelty and wafte. It was

was observed by one of the Chiefs of *Sky*, that fifty armed men might, without resistance, ravage the country. Laws that place the subjects in such a state, contravene the first principles of the compact of authority: they exact obedience, and yield no protection.

It affords a generous and manly pleasure to conceive a little nation gathering its fruits and tending its herds with fearless confidence, though it lies open on every side to invasion, where, in contempt of walls and trenches, every man sleeps securely with his sword beside him; where all on the first approach of hostility came together at the call to battle, as at a summons to a festal show; and committing their cattle to the care of those whom age or nature has disabled, engage the enemy with that competition for hazard and for glory, which operate in men that fight under the eye of those, whose dislike or kindness they have always considered as the greatest evil or the greatest good.

This was, in the beginning of the present century, the state of the Highlands. Every man was a soldier, who partook of national confidence, and interested himself in national honour. To lose this spirit, is to lose what no small advantage will compensate.

It may likewise deserve to be inquired, whether a great nation ought to be totally commercial? whether, amidst the uncertainty of human affairs, too much attention to one mode of happiness may not endanger others? whether the pride of riches must not sometimes have recourse to the protection of courage? and whether, if it be necessary to preserve in some part of the empire the military spirit, it can subsist more commodiously in any place, than in remote and unprofitable provinces, where it can commonly do little harm, and whence it may be called forth at any sudden exigence?

It must however be confessed, that a man who places honour only in succesful violence, is a very troublesome and pernicious animal in time of peace; and that the martial character cannot prevail in a whole people, but by the diminution of all other virtues. He that is accustomed to resolve all right into conquest, will have very little tenderness or equity. All the friendship in such a life can only be a confederacy of invasion, or alliance of defence. The strong must flourish by force, and the weak subsist by stratagem.

Till the Highlanders lost their ferocity, with their arms, they suffered from each other all that malignity could dictate, or precipitance could act. Every provocation was revenged with blood, and no man that ventured into a numerous company, by whatever occasion brought together, was sure of returning without a wound. If they are now exposed to foreign hostilities, they may talk of the danger, but can seldom feel it. If they are no longer martial, they are no longer quarrelsome. Misery is caused for the most part, not by a heavy crush of disaster, but by the corrosion of less visible evils, which canker enjoyment, and undermine security. The visit of an invader is necessarily rare, but domestick animosities allow no cessation.

The abolition of the local jurisdictions, which had for so many ages been exercised by the Chiefs, has likewise its evil and its good. The feudal constitution naturally diffused itself into long ramifications of subordinate authority. To this general temper of the government was added the peculiar form of the country, broken by mountains into many subdivisions scarcely accessible

acceſſible but to the natives, and guarded by paſſes, or perplexed with intricacies, through which national juſtice could not find its way.

The power of deciding controverſies, and of puniſhing offences, as ſome ſuch power there muſt always be, was entruſted to the Lairds of the country, to thoſe whom the people conſidered as their natural judges. It cannot be ſuppoſed that a rugged proprietor of the rocks, unprincipled and unenlightened, was a nice reſolver of entangled claims, or very exact in proportioning puniſhment to offences. But the more he indulged his own will, the more he held his vaſſals in dependance. Prudence and innocence, without the favour of the Chief, conferred no ſecurity; and crimes involved no danger, when the judge was reſolute to acquit.

When the Chiefs were men of knowledge and virtue, the convenience of a domestick judicature was great. No long journies were necessary, nor artificial delays could be practised; the character, the alliances, and interests of the litigants were known to the court, and all false pretences were easily detected. The sentence, when it was past, could not be evaded; the power of the Laird superseded formalities, and justice could not be defeated by interest or stratagem.

I doubt not but that since the regular judges have made their circuits through the whole country, right has been every where more wisely and more equally distributed; the complaint is, that litigation is grown troublesome, and that the magistrates are too few, and therefore often too remote for general convenience.

Many

Many of the smaller Islands have no legal officer within them. I once asked, If a crime should be committed, by what authority the offender could be seized? and was told, that the Laird would exert his right; a right which he must now usurp, but which surely necessity must vindicate, and which is therefore yet exercised in lower degrees by some of the proprietors, when legal processes cannot be obtained.

In all greater questions, however, there is now happily an end to all fear or hope from malice or from favour. The roads are secure in those places through which, forty years ago, no traveller could pass without a convoy. All trials of right by the sword are forgotten, and the mean are in as little danger from the powerful as in other places. No scheme of policy has, in any country, yet brought the rich and poor on equal terms into courts of judicature.

ture. Perhaps experience, improving on experience, may in time effect it.

Those who have long enjoyed dignity and power, ought not to lose it without some equivalent. There was paid to the Chiefs by the publick, in exchange for their privileges, perhaps a sum greater than most of them had ever possessed, which excited a thirst for riches, of which it shewed them the use. When the power of birth and station ceases, no hope remains but from the prevalence of money. Power and wealth supply the place of each other. Power confers the ability of gratifying our desire without the consent of others. Wealth enables us to obtain the consent of others to our gratification. Power, simply considered, whatever it confers on one, must take from another. Wealth enables its owner to give to others, by taking only from himself. Power pleases the violent and proud: wealth delights the placid

placid and the timorous. Youth therefore flies at power, and age grovels after riches.

The Chiefs, divested of their prerogatives, necessarily turned their thoughts to the improvement of their revenues, and expect more rent, as they have less homage. The tenant, who is far from perceiving that his condition is made better in the same proportion, as that of his landlord is made worse, does not immediately see why his industry is to be taxed more heavily than before. He refuses to pay the demand, and is ejected; the ground is then let to a stranger, who perhaps brings a larger stock, but who, taking the land at its full price, treats with the Laird upon equal terms, and considers him not as a Chief, but as a trafficker in land. Thus the estate perhaps is improved, but the Clan is broken.

It

It seems to be the general opinion, that the rents have been raised with too much eagerness. Some regard must be paid to prejudice. Those who have hitherto paid but little, will not suddenly be persuaded to pay much, though they can afford it. As ground is gradually improved, and the value of money decreases, the rent may be raised without any diminution of the farmer's profits: yet it is necessary in these countries, where the ejection of a tenant is a greater evil, than in more populous places, to consider not merely what the land will produce, but with what ability the inhabitant can cultivate it. A certain stock can allow but a certain payment; for if the land be doubled, and the stock remains the same, the tenant becomes no richer. The proprietors of the Highlands might perhaps often increase their income, by subdividing the farms, and allotting to every occupier only so many acres as he can profitably employ, but that they want people.

There

There seems now, whatever be the cause, to be through a great part of the Highlands a general discontent. That adherence, which was lately professed by every man to the Chief of his name, has now little prevalence; and he that cannot live as he desires at home, listens to the tale of fortunate islands and happy regions, where every man may have land of his own, and eat the product of his labour without a superior.

Those who have obtained grants of American lands, have, as is well known, invited settlers from all quarters of the globe; and among other places, where oppression might produce a wish for new habitations, their emissaries would not fail to try their persuasions in the Isles of Scotland, where at the time when the Clans were newly disunited from their Chiefs, and exasperated by unprecedented exactions, it is no wonder that they prevailed.

Whether

Whether the mischiefs of emigration were immediately perceived, may be justly questioned. They who went first, were probably such as could best be spared; but the accounts sent by the earliest adventurers, whether true or false, inclined many to follow them; and whole neighbourhoods formed parties for removal; so that departure from their native country is no longer exile. He that goes thus accompanied, carries with him all that makes life pleasant. He sits down in a better climate, surrounded by his kindred and his friends: they carry with them their language, their opinions, their popular songs, and hereditary merriment: they change nothing but the place of their abode; and of that change they perceive the benefit.

This is the real effect of emigration, if those that go away together settle on the same spot, and preserve their ancient union. But some relate that these adventurous visitants

ants of unknown regions, after a voyage passed in dreams of plenty and felicity, are dispersed at last upon a sylvan wilderness, where their first years must be spent in toil, to clear the ground which is afterwards to be tilled, and that the whole effect of their undertaking is only more fatigue and equal scarcity.

Both accounts may be suspected. Those who are gone will endeavour by every art to draw others after them; for as their numbers are greater, they will provide better for themselves. When *Nova Scotia* was first peopled, I remember a letter, published under the character of a New Planter, who related how much the climate put him in mind of Italy. Such intelligence the *Hebridians* probably receive from their transmarine correspondents. But with equal temptations of interest, and perhaps with no greater niceness of veracity, the owners of the Islands spread stories of American hardships

hardships to keep their people content at home.

Some method to stop this epidemick desire of wandering, which spreads its contagion from valley to valley, deserves to be sought with great diligence. In more fruitful countries, the removal of one, only makes room for the succession of another: but in the *Hebrides*, the loss of an inhabitant leaves a lasting vacuity; for nobody born in any other parts of the world will choose this country for his residence; and an Island once depopulated will remain a desert, as long as the present facility of travel gives every one, who is discontented and unsettled, the choice of his abode.

Let it be inquired, whether the first intention of those who are fluttering on the wing, and collecting a flock that they may take their flight, be to attain good, or to avoid evil. If they are dissatisfied

fied with that part of the globe, which their birth has allotted them, and resolve not to live without the pleasures of happier climates; if they long for bright suns, and calm skies, and flowery fields, and fragrant gardens, I know not by what eloquence they can be persuaded, or by what offers they can be hired, to stay.

But if they are driven from their native country by positive evils, and disgusted by ill-treatment, real or imaginary, it were fit to remove their grievances, and quiet their resentment; since, if they have been hitherto undutiful subjects, they will not much mend their principles by American conversation.

To allure them into the army, it was thought proper to indulge them in the continuance of their national dress. If this concession could have any effect, it might easily be made. That dissimilitude of appearance,

pearance, which was supposed to keep them distinct from the rest of the nation, might disincline them from coalescing with the *Pensylvanians* or people of *Connecticut*. If the restitution of their arms will reconcile them to their country, let them have again those weapons, which will not be more mischievous at home than in the Colonies. That they may not fly from the increase of rent, I know not whether the general good does not require that the landlords be, for a time, restrained in their demands, and kept quiet by pensions proportionate to their loss.

To hinder insurrection by driving away the people, and to govern peaceably by having no subjects, is an expedient that argues no great profundity of politicks. To soften the obdurate, to convince the mistaken, to mollify the resentful, are worthy of a statesman; but it affords a legislator little self-applause to consider, that where

where there was formerly an infurrection, there is now a wildernefs.

It has been a queftion often agitated without folution, why thofe northern regions are now fo thinly peopled, which formerly overwhelmed with their armies the Roman empire. The queftion fuppofes what I believe is not true, that they had once more inhabitants than they could maintain, and overflowed only becaufe they were full.

This is to eftimate the manners of all countries and ages by our own. Migration, while the ftate of life was unfettled, and there was little communication of intelligence between diftant places, was among the wilder nations of Europe, capricious and cafual. An adventitious projector heard of a fertile coaft unoccupied, and led out a colony; a chief of renown for bravery, called the young men together, and led them out to try what fortune would prefent. When Cæfar was

was in *Gaul*, he found the Helvetians preparing to go they knew not whither, and put a ſtop to their motions. They ſettled again in their own country, where they were ſo far from wanting room, that they had accumulated three years proviſion for their march.

The religion of the North was military; if they could not find enemies, it was their duty to make them: they travelled in queſt of danger, and willing(took the chance of Empire or Death. If their troops were numerous, the countries from which they were collected are of vaſt extent, and without much exuberance of people great armies may be raiſed where every man is a ſoldier. But their true numbers were never known. Thoſe who were conquered by them are their hiſtorians, and ſhame may have excited them to ſay, that they were overwhelmed with multitudes. To count is a modern practice, the ancient method

method was to guefs; and when numbers are guessed they are always magnified.

Thus England has for several years been filled with the atchievements of seventy thousand Highlanders employed in *America*. I have heard from an English officer, not much inclined to favour them, that their behaviour deserved a very high degree of military praise; but their number has been much exaggerated. One of the ministers told me, that seventy thousand men could not have been found in all the Highlands, and that more than twelve thousand never took the field. Those that went to the American war, went to destruction. Of the old Highland regiment, consisting of twelve hundred, only seventy-six survived to see their country again.

The Gothick swarms have at least been multiplied with equal liberality. That they bore no great proportion to the inhabitants, in whose countries they settled, is plain from

That the immediate motives of their defertion muft be imputed to their landlords, may be reafonably concluded, becaufe fome Lairds of more prudence and lefs rapacity have kept their vaffals undiminifhed. From *Raafay* only one man had been feduced, and at *Col* there was no wifh to go away.

The traveller who comes hither from more opulent countries, to fpeculate upon the remains of paftoral life, will not much wonder that a common Highlander has no ftrong adherence to his native foil; for of animal enjoyments, or of phyfical good, he leaves nothing that he may not find again wherefoever he may be thrown.

The habitations of men in the *Hebrides* may be diftinguifhed into huts and houfes. By a *houfe*, I mean a building with one ftory over another; by a *hut*, a dwelling with only one floor. The Laird, who formerly

merly lived in a caſtle, now lives in a houſe; ſometimes ſufficiently neat, but ſeldom very ſpacious or ſplendid. The Tackſmen and the Miniſters have commonly houſes. Wherever there is a houſe, the ſtranger finds a welcome, and to the other evils of exterminating Tackſmen may be added the unavoidable ceſſation of hoſpitality, or the devolution of too heavy a burden on the Miniſters.

Of the houſes little can be ſaid. They are ſmall, and by the neceſſity of accumulating ſtores, where there are ſo few opportunities of purchaſe, the rooms are very heterogeneouſly filled. With want of cleanlineſs it were ingratitude to reproach them. The ſervants having been bred upon the naked earth, think every floor clean, and the quick ſucceſſion of gueſts, perhaps not always over-elegant, does not allow much time for adjuſting their apartments.

Huts are of many gradations; from murky dens, to commodious dwellings.

The wall of a common hut is always built without mortar, by a skilful adaptation of loose stones. Sometimes perhaps a double wall of stones is raised, and the intermediate space filled with earth. The air is thus completely excluded. Some walls are, I think, formed of turfs, held together by a wattle, or texture of twigs. Of the meanest huts, the first room is lighted by the entrance, and the second by the smoke-hole. The fire is usually made in the middle. But there are huts, or dwellings, of only one story, inhabited by gentlemen, which have walls cemented with mortar, glass windows, and boarded floors. Of these all have chimneys, and some chimneys have grates.

The house and the furniture are not always nicely suited. We were driven once,

once, by miffing a paffage, to the hut of a gentleman, where, after a very liberal fupper, when I was conducted to my chamber, I found an elegant bed of Indian cotton, fpread with fine fheets. The accommodation was flattering; I undreffed myfelf, and felt my feet in the mire. The bed ftood upon the bare earth, which a long courfe of rain had foftened to a puddle.

In paftoral countries the condition of the loweft rank of people is fufficiently wretched. Among manufacturers, men that have no property may have art and induftry, which make them neceffary, and therefore valuable. But where flocks and corn are the only wealth, there are always more hands than work, and of that work there is little in which fkill and dexterity can be much diftinguifhed. He therefore who is born poor never can be rich. The fon merely occupies the place of the father, and life

life knows nothing of progreſſion or advancement.

The petty tenants, and labouring peaſants, live in miſerable cabins, which afford them little more than ſhelter from the ſtorms. The Boor of *Norway* is ſaid to make all his own utenſils. In the *Hebrides*, whatever might be their ingenuity, the want of wood leaves them no materials. They are probably content with ſuch accommodations as ſtones of different forms and ſizes can afford them.

Their food is not better than their lodging. They ſeldom taſte the fleſh of land animals; for here are no markets. What each man eats is from his own ſtock. The great effect of money is to break property into ſmall parts. In towns, he that has a ſhilling may have a piece of meat; but where there is no commerce, no man can eat mutton but by killing a ſheep.

Fiſh

Fish in fair weather they need not want; but, I believe, man never lives long on fish, but by constraint; he will rather feed upon roots and berries.

The only fewel of the Islands is peat. Their wood is all consumed, and coal they have not yet found. Peat is dug out of the marshes, from the depth of one foot to that of six. That is accounted the best which is nearest the surface. It appears to be a mass of black earth held together by vegetable fibres. I know not whether the earth be bituminous, or whether the fibres be not the only combustible part; which, by heating the interposed earth red hot, make a burning mass. The heat is not very strong nor lasting. The ashes are yellowish, and in a large quantity. When they dig peat, they cut it into square pieces, and pile it up to dry beside the house. In some places it has an offensive smell. It is like wood charked for the smith. The
common

life knows nothing of progreſſion or advancement.

The petty tenants, and labouring peaſants, live in miſerable cabins, which afford them little more than ſhelter from the ſtorms. The Boor of *Norway* is ſaid to make all his own utenſils. In the *Hebrides*, whatever might be their ingenuity, the want of wood leaves them no materials. They are probably content with ſuch accommodations as ſtones of different forms and ſizes can afford them.

Their food is not better than their lodging. They ſeldom taſte the fleſh of land animals; for here are no markets. What each man eats is from his own ſtock. The great effect of money is to break property into ſmall parts. In towns, he that has a ſhilling may have a piece of meat; but where there is no commerce, no man can eat mutton but by killing a ſheep.

Fiſh

Fish in fair weather they need not want; but, I believe, man never lives long on fish, but by constraint; he will rather feed upon roots and berries.

The only fewel of the Islands is peat. Their wood is all consumed, and coal they have not yet found. Peat is dug out of the marshes, from the depth of one foot to that of six. That is accounted the best which is nearest the surface. It appears to be a mass of black earth held together by vegetable fibres. I know not whether the earth be bituminous, or whether the fibres be not the only combustible part; which, by heating the interposed earth red hot, make a burning mass. The heat is not very strong nor lasting. The ashes are yellowish, and in a large quantity. When they dig peat, they cut it into square pieces, and pile it up to dry beside the house. In some places it has an offensive smell. It is like wood charked for the smith. The common method of making peat fires, is by heaping it on the hearth; but it burns well in grates, and in the best houses is so used.

The common opinion is, that peat grows again where it has been cut; which, as it seems to be chiefly a vegetable substance, is not unlikely to be true, whether known or not to those who relate it.

There are water mills in *Sky* and *Raasay*; but where they are too far distant, the house-wives grind their oats with a quern, or hand-mill, which consists of two stones, about a foot and a half in diameter; the lower is a little convex, to which the concavity of the upper must be fitted. In the middle of the upper stone is a round hole, and on one side is a long handle. The grinder sheds the corn gradually into the hole with one hand, and works the handle round with the other. The corn slides

down

down the convexity of the lower stone, and by the motion of the upper is ground in its passage. These stones are found in *Lochabar*.

The Islands afford few pleasures, except to the hardy sportsman, who can tread the moor and climb the mountain. The distance of one family from another, in a country where travelling has so much difficulty, makes frequent intercourse impracticable. Visits last several days, and are commonly paid by water; yet I never saw a boat furnished with benches, or made commodious by any addition to the first fabrick. Conveniencies are not missed where they never were enjoyed.

The solace which the bagpipe can give, they have long enjoyed; but among other changes, which the last revolution introduced, the use of the bagpipe begins to be forgotten. Some of the chief families

still

still entertain a piper, whose office was anciently hereditary. *Macrimmon* was piper to *Macleod*, and *Rankin* to *Maclean* of *Col*.

The tunes of the bagpipe are traditional. There has been in *Sky*, beyond all time of memory, a college of pipers, under the direction of *Macrimmon*, which is not quite extinct. There was another in *Mull*, superintended by *Rankin*, which expired about sixteen years ago. To these colleges, while the pipe retained its honour, the students of musick repaired for education. I have had my dinner exhilarated by the bagpipe, at *Armidale*, at *Dunvegan*, and in *Col*.

The general conversation of the Islanders has nothing particular. I did not meet with the inquisitiveness of which I have read, and suspect the judgment to have been rashly made. A stranger of curiosity comes into a place where a stranger is seldom

dom feen: he importunes the people with queftions, of which they cannot guefs the motive, and gazes with furprife on things which they, having had them always before their eyes, do not fufpect of any thing wonderful. He appears to them like fome being of another world, and then thinks it peculiar that they take their turn to inquire whence he comes, and whither he is going.

The Iflands were long unfurnifhed with inftruction for youth, and none but the fons of gentlemen could have any literature. There are now parochial fchools, to which the lord of every manor pays a certain ftipend. Here the children are taught to read; but by the rule of their inftitution, they teach only *Englifh*, fo that the natives read a language which they may never ufe or underftand. If a parifh, which often happens, contains feveral Iflands, the fchool being but in one, cannot affift the reft.

rest. This is the state of *Col*, which, however, is more enlightened than some other places; for the deficiency is supplied by a young gentleman, who, for his own improvement, travels every year on foot over the Highlands to the session at Aberdeen; and at his return, during the vacation, teaches to read and write in his native Island.

In *Sky* there are two grammar schools, where boarders are taken to be regularly educated. The price of board is from three pounds, to four pounds ten shillings a year, and that of instruction is half a crown a quarter. But the scholars are birds of passage, who live at school only in the summer; for in winter provisions cannot be made for any considerable number in one place. This periodical dispersion impresses strongly the scarcity of these countries.

I heard

Having heard of no boarding-school for ladies nearer than *Inverness*, I suppose their education is generally domestick. The elder daughters of the higher families are sent into the world, and may contribute by their acquisitions to the improvement of the rest.

Women must here study to be either pleasing or useful. Their deficiencies are seldom supplied by very liberal fortunes. A hundred pounds is a portion beyond the hope of any but the Laird's daughter. They do not indeed often give money with their daughters; the question is, How many cows a young lady will bring her husband? A rich maiden has from ten to forty; but two cows are a decent fortune for one who pretends to no distinction.

The religion of the Islands is that of the Kirk of *Scotland*. The gentlemen with whom I conversed are all inclined to the

English

English liturgy; but they are obliged to maintain the established Minister, and the country is too poor to afford payment to another, who must live wholly on the contribution of his audience.

They therefore all attend the worship of the Kirk, as often as a visit from their Minister, or the practicability of travelling gives them opportunity; nor have they any reason to complain of insufficient pastors; for I saw not one in the Islands, whom I had reason to think either deficient in learning, or irregular in life; but found several with whom I could not converse without wishing, as my respect increased, that they had not been Presbyterians.

The ancient rigour of puritanism is now very much relaxed, though all are not yet equally enlightened. I sometimes met with prejudices sufficiently malignant, but they were prejudices of ignorance. The Ministers

Ministers in the Islands had attained such knowledge as may justly be admired in men, who have no motive to study, but generous curiosity, or, what is still better, desire of usefulness; with such politeness as so narrow a circle of converse could not have supplied; but to minds naturally disposed to elegance.

Reason and truth will prevail at last. The most learned of the Scottish Doctors would now gladly admit a form of prayer, if the people would endure it. The zeal or rage of congregations has its different degrees. In some parishes the Lord's Prayer is suffered: in others it is still rejected as a form; and he that should make it part of his supplication would be suspected of heretical pravity.

The principle upon which extemporary prayer was originally introduced, is no longer admitted. The Minister formerly, in the effusion of his prayer, expected immediate, and perhaps perceptible inspiration, and therefore thought it his duty not to think before what he should say. It is now universally confessed, that men pray as they speak on other occasions, according to the general measure of their abilities and attainments. Whatever each may think of a form prescribed by another, he cannot but believe that he can himself compose by study and meditation a better prayer than will rise in his mind at a sudden call; and if he has any hope of supernatural help, why may he not as well receive it when he writes as when he speaks?

In the variety of mental powers, some must perform extemporary prayer with much imperfection; and in the eagerness and rashness of contradictory opinions, if public liturgy be left to the private judgment of every Minister, the congre-

congregation may often be offended or misled.

There is in Scotland, as among ourselves, a restless suspicion of popish machinations, and a clamour of numerous converts to the Romish religion. The report is, I believe, in both parts of the Island equally false. The Romish religion is professed only in *Egg* and *Canna*, two small islands, into which the Reformation never made its way. If any missionaries are busy in the Highlands, their zeal entitles them to respect, even from those who cannot think favourably of their doctrine.

The political tenets of the Islanders I was not curious to investigate, and they were not eager to obtrude. Their conversation is decent and inoffensive. They disdain to drink for their principles, and there is no disaffection at their tables. I never heard a health offered by a Highlander that might

might not have circulated with propriety within the precincts of the King's palace.

Legal government has yet something of novelty to which they cannot perfectly conform. The ancient spirit that appealed only to the sword, is yet among them. The tenant of *Scalpa*, an island belonging to Macdonald, took no care to bring his rent; when the landlord talked of exacting payment, he declared his resolution to keep his ground, and drive all intruders from the Island, and continued to feed his cattle as on his own land, till it became necessary for the Sheriff to dislodge him by violence.

The various kinds of superstition which prevailed here, as in all other regions of ignorance, are by the diligence of the Ministers almost extirpated.

Of *Browny*, mentioned by Martin, nothing has been heard for many years. *Browny*

Browny was a sturdy Fairy; who, if he was fed, and kindly treated, would, as they said, do a great deal of work. They now pay him no wages, and are content to labour for themselves.

In *Troda*, within these three-and-thirty years, milk was put every Saturday for *Greogach*, or *the Old Man with the Long Beard*. Whether *Greogach* was courted as kind, or dreaded as terrible, whether they meant, by giving him the milk, to obtain good, or avert evil, I was not informed. The Minister is now living by whom the practice was abolished.

They have still among them a great number of charms for the cure of different diseases; they are all invocations, perhaps transmitted to them from the times of popery, which increasing knowledge will bring into disuse.

They have opinions, which cannot be ranked with superstition, because they regard only natural effects. They expect better crops of grain, by sowing their seed in the moon's increase. The moon has great influence in vulgar philosophy. In my memory it was a precept annually given in one of the *English* Almanacks, *to kill hogs when the moon was increasing, and the bacon would prove the better in boiling.*

We should have had little claim to the praise of curiosity, if we had not endeavoured with particular attention to examine the question of the *Second Sight*. Of an opinion received for centuries by a whole nation, and supposed to be confirmed through its whole descent, by a series of successive facts, it is desirable that the truth should be established, or the fallacy detected.

The *Second Sight* is an impression made either by the mind upon the eye, or by the eye upon the mind, by which things distant or future are perceived, and seen as if they
were

were prefent. A man on a journey far from home falls from his horfe, another, who is perhaps at work about the houfe, fees him bleeding on the ground, commonly with a landfcape of the place where the accident befalls him. Another feer, driving home his cattle, or wandering in idlenefs, or mufing in the funfhine, is fuddenly furprifed by the appearance of a bridal ceremony, or funeral proceffion, and counts the mourners or attendants, of whom, if he knows them, he relates the names, if he knows them not, he can defcribe the dreffes. Things diftant are feen at the inftant when they happen. Of things future I know not that there is any rule for determining the time between the Sight and the event.

This receptive faculty, for power it cannot be called, is neither voluntary nor conftant. The appearances have no dependence upon choice: they cannot be
 fummoned,

summoned, detained, or recalled. The impreffion is fudden, and the effect often painful.

By the term *Second Sight*, feems to be meant a mode of feeing, fuperadded to that which Nature generally beftows, In the *Earfe* it is called *Taifch*; which fignifies likewife a fpectre, or a vifion. I know not, nor is it likely that the Highlanders ever examined, whether by *Taifch*, ufed for *Second Sight*, they mean the power of feeing, or the thing feen.

I do not find it to be true, as it is reported, that to the *Second Sight* nothing is prefented but phantoms of evil. Good feems to have the fame proportion in thofe vifionary fcenes, as it obtains in real life: almoft all remarkable events have evil for their bafis; and are either miferies incurred, or miferies efcaped. Our fenfe is fo much ftronger of what we fuffer, than of

what

what we enjoy, that the ideas of pain predominate in almost every mind. What is recollection but a revival of vexations, or history but a record of wars, treasons, and calamities? Death, which is considered as the greatest evil, happens to all. The greatest good, be it what it will, is the lot but of a part.

That they should often see death is to be expected; because death is an event frequent and important. But they see likewise more pleasing incidents. A gentleman told me, that when he had once gone far from his own Island, one of his labouring servants predicted his return, and described the livery of his attendant, which he had never worn at home; and which had been, without any previous design, occasionally given him.

Our desire of information was keen, and our inquiry frequent. Mr. Boswell's frankness

ness and gaiety made every body communicative; and we heard many tales of these airy shows, with more or less evidence and distinctness.

It is the common talk of the Lowland *Scots*, that the notion of the *Second Sight* is wearing away with other superstitions; and that its reality is no longer supposed, but by the grossest people. How far its prevalence ever extended, or what ground it has lost, I know not. The Islanders of all degrees, whether of rank or understanding, universally admit it, except the Ministers, who universally deny it, and are suspected to deny it, in consequence of a system, against conviction. One of them honestly told me, that he came to *Sky* with a resolution not to believe it.

Strong reasons for incredulity will readily occur. This faculty of seeing things out of sight is local, and commonly useless. It is is a breach of the common order of things, without any visible reason or perceptible benefit. It is ascribed only to a people very little enlightened; and among them, for the most part, to the mean and the ignorant.

To the confidence of these objections it may be replied, that by presuming to determine what is fit, and what is beneficial, they presuppose more knowledge of the universal system than man has attained; and therefore depend upon principles too complicated and extensive for our comprehension; and that there can be no security in the consequence, when the premises are not understood; that the *Second Sight* is only wonderful because it is rare, for considered in itself, it involves no more difficulty than dreams, or perhaps than the regular exercise of the cogitative faculty; that a general opinion of communicative impulses, or visionary representations, has
prevailed

prevailed in all ages and all nations; that particular inftances have been given, with fuch evidence, as neither *Bacon* nor *Bayle* has been able to refift; that fudden impreffions, which the event has verified, have been felt by more than own or publifh them; that the *Second Sight* of the *Hebrides* implies only the local frequency of a power, which is no where totally unknown; and that where we are unable to decide by antecedent reafon, we muft be content to yield to the force of teftimony.

By pretenfion to *Second Sight*, no profit was ever fought or gained. It is an involuntary affection, in which neither hope nor fear are known to have any part. Thofe who profefs to feel it, do not boaft of it as a privilege, nor are confidered by others as advantageoufly diftinguifhed. They have no temptation to feign; and their hearers have no motive to encourage the impofture.

To talk with any of these seers is not easy. There is one living in *Sky*, with whom we would have gladly conversed; but he was very grofs and ignorant, and knew no *English*. The proportion in these countries of the poor to the rich is such, that if we suppose the quality to be accidental, it can very rarely happen to a man of education; and yet on such men it has sometimes fallen. There is now a Second Sighted gentleman in the Highlands, who complains of the terrors to which he is exposed.

The foresight of the Seers is not always prescience: they are impressed with images, of which the event only shews them the meaning. They tell what they have seen to others, who are at that time not more knowing than themselves, but may become at last very adequate witnesses, by comparing the narrative with its verification.

To

To collect sufficient testimonies for the satisfaction of the publick, or of ourselves, would have required more time than we could bestow. There is, against it, the seeming analogy of things confusedly seen, and little understood; and for it, the indistinct cry of national persuasion, which may be perhaps resolved at last into prejudice and tradition. I never could advance my curiosity to conviction; but came away at last only willing to believe.

As there subsists no longer in the Islands much of that peculiar and discriminative form of life, of which the idea had delighted our imagination, we were willing to listen to such accounts of past times as would be given us. But we soon found what memorials were to be expected from an illiterate people, whose whole time is a series of distress; where every morning is labouring with expedients for the evening; and where all mental pains or pleasure arose

from

from the dread of winter, the expectation of spring, the caprices of their Chiefs, and the motions of the neighbouring Clans; where there was neither shame from ignorance, nor pride in knowledge; neither curiosity to inquire, nor vanity to communicate.

The Chiefs indeed were exempt from urgent penury, and daily difficulties; and in their houses were preserved what accounts remained of past ages. But the Chiefs were sometimes ignorant and careless, and sometimes kept busy by turbulence and contention; and one generation of ignorance effaces the whole series of unwritten history. Books are faithful repositories, which may be a while neglected or forgotten; but when they are opened again, will again impart their instruction: memory, once interrupted, is not to be recalled. Written learning is a fixed luminary, which, after the cloud that had hidden it has paſt away, is again bright in its proper ſtation. Tradition is but a meteor, which, if once it falls, cannot be rekindled.

It ſeems to be univerſally ſuppoſed, that much of the local hiſtory was preſerved by the Bards, of whom one is ſaid to have been retained by every great family. After theſe Bards were ſome of my firſt inquiries; and I received ſuch anſwers as, for a while, made me pleaſe myſelf with my increaſe of knowledge; for I had not then learned how to eſtimate the narration of a Highlander.

They ſaid that a great family had a *Bard* and a *Senachi*, who were the poet and hiſtorian of the houſe; and an old gentleman told me that he remembered one of each. Here was a dawn of intelligence. Of men that had lived within memory, ſome certain knowledge might be attained. Though the office had ceaſed, its effects might

might continue; the poems might be found though there was no poet.

Another converfation indeed informed me, that the fame man was both Bard and Senachi. This variation difcouraged me; but as the practice might be different in different times, or at the fame time in different families, there was yet no reafon for fuppofing that I muft neceffarily fit down in total ignorance.

Soon after I was told by a gentleman who is generally acknowledged the greateft mafter of *Hebridian* antiquities, that there had indeed once been both Bards and Senachies; and that *Senachi* fignified *the man of talk*, or of converfation; but that neither Bard nor Senachi had exifted for fome centuries. I have no reafon to fuppofe it exactly known at what time the cuftom ceafed, nor did it probably ceafe in all houfes at once. But whenever the practice of recitation was difused, the works, whether poetical or historical, perished with the authors; for in those times nothing had been written in the *Earse* language.

Whether the *Man of talk* was a historian, whose office was to tell truth, or a story-teller, like those which were in the last century, and perhaps are now among the Irish, whose trade was only to amuse, it now would be vain to inquire.

Most of the domestick offices were, I believe, hereditary; and probably the laureat of a Clan was always the son of the last laureat. The history of the race could no otherwise be communicated, or retained; but what genius could be expected in a poet by inheritance?

The nation was wholly illiterate. Neither Bards nor Senachies could write or read; but if they were ignorant, there was no danger

danger of detection; they were believed by those whose vanity they flattered.

The recital of genealogies, which has been considered as very efficacious to the preservation of a true series of ancestry, was anciently made, when the heir of the family came to manly age. This practice has never subsisted within time of memory, nor was much credit due to such rehearsers, who might obtrude fictitious pedigrees, either to please their masters, or to hide the deficiency of their own memories.

Where the Chiefs of the Highlands have found the histories of their descent is difficult to tell; for no *Earse* genealogy was ever written. In general this only is evident, that the principal house of a clan must be very ancient, and that those must have lived long in a place, of whom it is not known when they came thither.

Thus hopeless are all attempts to find any traces of Highland learning. Nor are their primitive customs and ancient manner of life otherwise than very faintly and uncertainly remembered by the present race.

The peculiarities which strike the native of a commercial country, proceeded in a great measure from the want of money. To the servants and dependants that were not domesticks, and if an estimate be made from the capacity of any of their old houses which I have seen, their domesticks could have been but few, were appropriated certain portions of land for their support. *Macdonald* has a piece of ground yet, called the Bards or Senachies field. When a beef was killed for the house, particular parts were claimed as fees by the several officers, or workmen. What was the right of each I have not learned. The head belonged to the smith, and the udder of a cow to the piper:

piper; the weaver had likewife his particular part; and fo many pieces followed thefe prefcriptive claims, that the Laird's was at laft but little.

The payment of rent in kind has been fo long difufed in England, that it is totally forgotten. It was practifed very lately in the *Hebrides*, and probably ftill continues, not only in *St. Kilda*, where money is not yet known, but in others of the fmaller and remoter Iflands. It were perhaps to be defired, that no change in this particular fhould have been made. When the Laird could only eat the produce of his lands, he was under the neceffity of refiding upon them; and when the tenant could not convert his ftock into more portable riches, he could never be tempted away from his farm, from the only place where he could be wealthy. Money confounds fubordination, by overpowering the diftinctions of rank and birth, and weakens authority by supplying power of resistance, or expedients for escape. The feudal system is formed for a nation employed in agriculture, and has never long kept its hold where gold and silver have become common.

Their arms were anciently the *Glaymore*, or great two-handed sword, and afterwards the two-edged sword and target, or buckler, which was sustained on the left arm. In the midst of the target, which was made of wood, covered with leather, and studded with nails, a slender lance, about two feet long, was sometimes fixed; it was heavy and cumberous, and accordingly has for some time past been gradually laid aside. Very few targets were at Culloden. The dirk, or broad dagger, I am afraid, was of more use in private quarrels than in battles. The Lochaber-ax is only a slight alteration of the old *English* bill.

After

After all that has been said of the force and terrour of the Highland sword, I could not find that the art of defence was any part of common education. The gentlemen were perhaps sometimes skilful gladiators, but the common men had no other powers than those of violence and courage. Yet it is well known, that the onset of the Highlanders was very formidable. As an army cannot consist of philosophers, a panick is easily excited by any unwonted mode of annoyance. New dangers are naturally magnified; and men accustomed only to exchange bullets at a distance, and rather to hear their enemies than see them, are discouraged and amazed when they find themselves encountered hand to hand, and catch the gleam of steel flashing in their faces.

The Highland weapons gave opportunity for many exertions of personal courage, and sometimes for single combats in

the

the field; like those which occur so frequently in fabulous wars. At Falkirk, a gentleman now living, was, I suppose after the retreat of the King's troops, engaged at a distance from the rest with an Irish dragoon. They were both skilful swordsmen, and the contest was not easily decided: the dragoon at last had the advantage, and the Highlander called for quarter; but quarter was refused him, and the fight continued till he was reduced to defend himself upon his knee. At that instant one of the Macleods came to his rescue; who, as it is said, offered quarter to the dragoon, but he thought himself obliged to reject what he had before refused, and, as battle gives little time to deliberate, was immediately killed.

Funerals were formerly solemnized by calling multitudes together, and entertaining them at great expence. This emulation of useless cost has been for some time discouraged,

raged, and at laſt in the Iſle of *Sky* is almoſt ſuppreſſed.

Of the Earſe language, as I underſtand nothing, I cannot ſay more than I have been told. It is the rude ſpeech of a barbarous people, who had few thoughts to expreſs, and were content, as they conceived groſsly, to be groſsly underſtood. After what has been lately talked of Highland Bards, and Highland genius, many will ſtartle when they are told, that the *Earſe* never was a written language; that there is not in the world an Earſe manuſcript a hundred years old; and that the ſounds of the Highlanders were never expreſſed by letters, till ſome little books of piety were tranſlated, and a metrical verſion of the Pſalms was made by the Synod of *Argyle*. Whoever therefore now writes in this language, ſpells according to his own perception of the ſound, and his own idea of the

power

power of the letters. The *Welsh* and the *Irish* are cultivated tongues. The Welsh, two hundred years ago, insulted their *English* neighbours for the instability of their Orthography; while the *Earse* merely floated in the breath of the people, and could therefore receive little improvement.

When a language begins to teem with books, it is tending to refinement; as those who undertake to teach others must have undergone some labour in improving themselves, they set a proportionate value on their own thoughts, and wish to enforce them by efficacious expressions; speech becomes embodied and permanent; different modes and phrases are compared, and the best obtains an establishment. By degrees one age improves upon another. Exactness is first obtained, and afterwards elegance. But diction, merely vocal, is always in its childhood. As no man leaves his

his eloquence behind him, the new generations have all to learn. There may poffibly be books without a polifhed language, but there can be no polifhed language without books.

That the Bards could not read more than the reft of their countrymen, it is reafonable to fuppofe; becaufe, if they had read, they could probably have written; and how high their compofitions may reafonably be rated, an inquirer may beft judge by confidering what ftores of imagery, what principles of ratiocination, what comprehenfion of knowledge, and what delicacy of elocution he has known any man attain who cannot read. The ftate of the Bards was yet more hopelefs. He that cannot read, may now converfe with thofe that can; but the Bard was a barbarian among barbarians, who, knowing nothing himfelf, lived with others that knew no more.

There has lately been in the Iflands one of thefe illiterate poets, who hearing the Bible read at church, is faid to have turned the facred hiftory into verfe. I heard part of a dialogue, compofed by him, tranflated by a young lady in *Mull*, and thought it had more meaning than I expected from a man totally uneducated; but he had fome opportunities of knowledge; he lived among a learned people. After all that has been done for the inftruction of the Highlanders, the antipathy between their language and literature ftill continues; and no man that has learned only *Earfe* is, at this time, able to read.

The *Earfe* has many dialects, and the words ufed in fome Iflands are not always known in others. In literate nations, though the pronunciation, and fometimes the words of common fpeech may differ, as now in *England*, compared with the South of *Scotland*, yet there is a written diction,

diction, which pervades all dialects, and is understood in every province. But where the whole language is colloquial, he that has only one part, never gets the rest, as he cannot get it but by change of residence.

In an unwritten speech, nothing that is not very short is transmitted from one generation to another. Few have opportunities of hearing a long composition often enough to learn it, or have inclination to repeat it so often as is necessary to retain it; and what is once forgotten is lost for ever. I believe there cannot be recovered, in the whole *Earse* language, five hundred lines of which there is any evidence to prove them a hundred years old. Yet I hear that the father of Ossian boasts of two chests more of ancient poetry, which he suppresses, because they are too good for the *English*.

He

He that goes into the Highlands with a mind naturally acquiescent, and a credulity eager for wonders, may come back with an opinion very different from mine; for the inhabitants knowing the ignorance of all strangers in their language and antiquities, perhaps are not very scrupulous adherents to truth; yet I do not say that they deliberately speak studied falsehood, or have a settled purpose to deceive. They have inquired and considered little, and do not always feel their own ignorance. They are not much accustomed to be interrogated by others; and seem never to have thought upon interrogating themselves; so that if they do not know what they tell to be true, they likewise do not distinctly perceive it to be false.

Mr. Boswell was very diligent in his inquiries; and the result of his investigations was, that the answer to the second question was

was commonly such as nullified the answer to the first.

We were a while told, that they had an old translation of the scriptures; and told it till it would appear obstinacy to inquire again. Yet by continued accumulation of questions we found, that the translation meant, if any meaning there were, was nothing else than the *Irish* Bible.

We heard of manuscripts that were, or that had been in the hands of somebody's father, or grandfather; but at last we had no reason to believe they were other than Irish. Martin mentions Irish, but never any Earse manuscripts, to be found in the Islands in his time.

I suppose my opinion of the poems of Ossian is already discovered. I believe they never existed in any other form than that which we have seen. The editor, or author, never could shew the original; nor can it be shewn by any other; to revenge

reasonable

reasonable incredulity, by refusing evidence, is a degree of insolence, with which the world is not yet acquainted; and stubborn audacity is the last refuge of guilt. It would be easy to shew it if he had it; but whence could it be had? It is too long to be remembered, and the language formerly had nothing written. He has doubtless inserted names that circulate in popular stories, and may have translated some wandering ballads, if any can be found; and the names, and some of the images being recollected, make an inaccurate auditor imagine, by the help of Caledonian bigotry, that he has formerly heard the whole.

I asked a very learned Minister in *Sky*, who had used all arts to make me believe the genuineness of the book, whether at last he believed it himself? but he would not answer. He wished me to be deceived, for the honour of his country; but would not directly and formally deceive me. Yet has this man's testimony been

been publickly produced, as of one that held Fingal to be the work of Ossian.

It is said, that some men of integrity profess to have heard parts of it, but they all heard them when they were boys; and it never was said that any of them could recite six lines. They remember names, and perhaps some proverbial sentiments; and, having no distinct ideas, coin a resemblance without an original. The persuasion of the Scots, however, is far from universal; and in a question so capable of proof, why should doubt be suffered to continue? The editor has been heard to say, that part of the poem was received by him, in the Saxon character. He has then found, by some peculiar fortune, an unwritten language, written in a character which the natives probably never beheld.

I have yet supposed no imposture but in the publisher; yet I am far from certainty, that some translations have not been lately made,

made, that may now be obtruded as parts of the original work. Credulity on one part is a strong temptation to deceit on the other, especially to deceit of which no personal injury is the consequence, and which flatters the author with his own ingenuity. The Scots have something to plead for their easy reception of an improbable fiction: they are seduced by their fondness for their supposed ancestors. A Scotchman must be a very sturdy moralist, who does not love *Scotland* better than truth; he will always love it better than inquiry; and if falsehood flatters his vanity, will not be very diligent to detect it. Neither ought the *English* to be much influenced by *Scotch* authority; for of the past and present state of the whole *Earse* nation, the Lowlanders are at least as ignorant as ourselves. To be ignorant is painful; but it is dangerous to quiet our uneasiness by the delusive opiate of hasty persuasion.

But

But this is the age in which those who could not read, have been supposed to write; in which the giants of antiquated romance have been exhibited as realities. If we know little of the ancient Highlanders, let us not fill the vacuity with *Ossian*. If we have not searched the *Magellanick* regions, let us however forbear to people them with *Patagons*.

Having waited some days at *Armidel*, we were flattered at last with a wind that promised to convey us to *Mull*. We went on board a boat that was taking in kelp, and left the Isle of *Sky* behind us. We were doomed to experience, like others, the danger of trusting to the wind, which blew against us, in a short time, with such violence, that we, being no seasoned sailors, were willing to call it a tempest. I was sea-sick and lay down. Mr. *Boswell* kept the deck. The master knew not well whither to go; and our difficulties might perhaps have filled a very pathetick page, had not Mr. *Maclean* of *Col*, who, with every other qualification which infular life requires, is a very active and fkilful mariner, piloted us fafe into his own harbour.

C O L.

In the morning we found ourfelves under the Ifle of *Col*, where we landed; and paffed the firft day and night with Captain *Maclean*, a gentleman who has lived fome time in the Eaft Indies; but having dethroned no Nabob, is not too rich to fettle in his own country.

Next day the wind was fair, and we might have had an eafy paffage to *Mull*; but having, contrarily to our own intention, landed upon a new Ifland, we would not leave it wholly unexamined. We therefore fuffered the veffel to depart without us, and trufted the fkies for another wind.

Mr. *Maclean* of *Col*, having a very numerous family, has, for fome time paft,
refided

resided at *Aberdeen*, that he may superintend their education, and leaves the young gentleman, our friend, to govern his dominions, with the full power of a Highland Chief. By the absence of the Laird's family, our entertainment was made more difficult, because the house was in a great degree disfurnished; but young *Col*'s kindness and activity supplied all defects, and procured us more than sufficient accommodation.

Here I first mounted a little Highland steed; and if there had been many spectators, should have been somewhat ashamed of my figure in the march. The horses of the Islands, as of other barren countries, are very low: they are indeed musculous and strong, beyond what their size gives reason for expecting; but a bulky man upon one of their backs makes a very disproportionate appearance.

From the habitation of Captain *Maclean*, we went to *Grissipol*, but called by the way on Mr. *Hector Maclean*, the Minister of *Col*, whom we found in a hut, that is, a house of only one floor, but with windows and chimney, and not inelegantly furnished. Mr. *Maclean* has the reputation of great learning: he is seventy-seven years old, but not infirm, with a look of venerable dignity, excelling what I remember in any other man.

His conversation was not unsuitable to his appearance. I lost some of his goodwill, by treating a heretical writer with more regard than, in his opinion, a heretick could deserve. I honoured his orthodoxy, and did not much censure his asperity. A man who has settled his opinions, does not love to have the tranquillity of his conviction disturbed; and at seventy-seven it is time to be in earnest.

Men-

Mention was made of the *Earſe* tranſlation of the New Teſtament, which has been lately publiſhed, and of which the learned Mr. *Macqueen* of *Sky* ſpoke with commendation; but Mr. *Maclean* ſaid he did not uſe it, becauſe he could make the text more intelligible to his auditors by an extemporary verſion. From this I inferred, that the language of the tranſlation was not the language of the Iſle of *Col*.

He has no publick edifice for the exerciſe of his miniſtry; and can officiate to no greater number, than a room can contain; and the room of a hut is not very large. This is all the opportunity of worſhip that is now granted to the inhabitants of the Iſland, ſome of whom muſt travel thither perhaps ten miles. Two chapels were erected by their anceſtors, of which I ſaw the ſkeletons, which now ſtand faithful witneſſes of the triumph of Reformation.

The

The want of churches is not the only impediment to piety: there is likewise a want of Ministers. A parish often contains more Islands than one; and each Island can have the Minister only in its own turn. At *Raasa* they had, I think, a right to service only every third Sunday. All the provision made by the present ecclesiastical constitution, for the inhabitants of about a hundred square miles, is a prayer and sermon in a little room, once in three weeks: and even this parsimonious distribution is at the mercy of the weather: and in those Islands where the Minister does not reside, it is impossible to tell how many weeks or months may pass without any publick exercise of religion.

GRISSIPOL IN COL.

After a short conversation with Mr. *Maclean*, we went on to *Grissipol*, a house and farm tenanted by Mr. *Macsweyn*, where I saw

saw more of the ancient life of a Highlander, than I had yet found. Mrs. *Macfweyn* could fpeak no *Englifh*, and had never feen any other places than the Iflands of *Sky*, *Mull*, and *Col:* but fhe was hofpitable and good-humoured, and fpread her table with fufficient liberality. We found tea here, as in every other place, but our fpoons were of horn.

The houfe of *Griffipol* ftands by a brook very clear and quick; which is, I fuppofe, one of the moft copious ftreams in the Ifland. This place was the fcene of an action, much celebrated in the traditional hiftory of *Col*, but which probably no two relaters will tell alike.

Some time, in the obfcure ages, *Macneil* of *Barra* married the Lady *Maclean*, who had the Ifle of *Col* for her jointure. Whether *Macneil* detained *Col*, when the widow was dead, or whether fhe lived fo

long

long as to make her heirs impatient, is perhaps not now known. The younger son, called *John Gerves*, or *John the Giant*, a man of great strength, who was then in *Ireland*, either for safety, or for education, dreamed of recovering his inheritance; and getting some adventurers together, which in those unsettled times was not hard to do, invaded *Col*. He was driven away, but was not discouraged, and collecting new followers, in three years came again with fifty men. In his way he stopped at *Artorinish* in *Morvern*, where his uncle was prisoner to *Macleod*, and was then with his enemies in a tent. *Maclean* took with him only one servant, whom he ordered to stay at the outside; and where he should see the tent pressed outwards, to strike with his dirk; it being the intention of *Maclean*, as any man provoked him, to lay hands upon him, and push him back. He entered the tent alone, with his *Lochabar-axe* in his hand, and struck such terror into

into the whole assembly, that they dismissed his uncle.

When he landed at *Col*, he saw the sentinel, who kept watch towards the sea, running off to *Grissipol*, to give *Macneil*, who was there with a hundred and twenty men, an account of the invasion. He told *Macgill*, one of his followers, that if he intercepted that dangerous intelligence, by catching the courier, he would give him certain lands in *Mull*. Upon this promise, *Macgill* pursued the messenger, and either killed, or stopped him; and his posterity, till very lately, held the lands in *Mull*.

The alarm being thus prevented, he came unexpectedly upon *Macneil*. Chiefs were in those days never wholly unprovided for an enemy. A fight ensued, in which one of their followers is said to have given an extraordinary proof of activity, by bound-

ing

ing backwards over the brook of *Griſſipol.* *Macneil* being killed, and many of his clan deſtroyed, *Maclean* took poſſeſſion of the Iſland, which the *Macneils* attempted to conquer by another invaſion, but were defeated and repulſed.

Maclean, in his turn, invaded the eſtate of the *Macneils,* took the caſtle of *Brecacig,* and conquered the Iſle of *Barra,* which he held for ſeven years, and then reſtored it to the heirs.

CASTLE OF COL.

From *Griſſipol,* Mr. *Maclean* conducted us to his father's ſeat; a neat new houſe, erected near the old caſtle, I think, by the laſt proprietor. Here we were allowed to take our ſtation, and lived very commodiouſly, while we waited for moderate weather and a fair wind, which we did not ſo ſoon obtain, but we had time to get

ſome

some information of the present state of *Col*, partly by inquiry, and partly by occasional excursions.

Col is computed to be thirteen miles in length, and three in breadth. Both the ends are the property of the Duke of *Argyle*, but the middle belongs to *Maclean*, who is called *Col*, as the only Laird.

Col is not properly rocky; it is rather one continued rock, of a surface much diversified with protuberances, and covered with a thin layer of earth, which is often broken, and discovers the stone. Such a soil is not for plants that strike deep roots; and perhaps in the whole Island nothing has ever yet grown to the height of a table. The uncultivated parts are clothed with heath, among which industry has interspersed spots of grass and corn; but no attempt has yet been made to raise a tree. Young *Col*, who has a very laudable desire of of improving his patrimony, purposes some time to plant an orchard; which, if it be sheltered by a wall, may perhaps succeed. He has introduced the culture of turnips, of which he has a field, where the whole work was performed by his own hand. His intention is to provide food for his cattle in the winter. This innovation was considered by Mr. *Macsweyn* as the idle project of a young head, heated with *English* fancies; but he has now found that turnips will really grow, and that hungry sheep and cows will really eat them.

By such acquisitions as these, the *Hebrides* may in time rise above their annual distress. Wherever heath will grow, there is reason to think something better may draw nourishment; and by trying the production of other places, plants will be found suitable to every soil.

Col has many lochs, some of which have trouts and eels, and others have never yet been

been stocked; another proof of the negligence of the Islanders, who might take fish in the inland waters, when they cannot go to sea.

Their quadrupeds are horses, cows, sheep, and goats. They have neither deer, hares, nor rabbits. They have no vermin, except rats, which have been lately brought thither by sea, as to other places; and are free from serpents, frogs, and toads.

The harvest in *Col*, and in *Lewis*, is ripe sooner than in *Sky*, and the winter in *Col* is never cold, but very tempestuous. I know not that I ever heard the wind so loud in any other place; and Mr. *Boswell* observed, that its noise was all its own, for there were no trees to increase it.

Noise is not the worst effect of the tempests; for they have thrown the sand from the shore over a considerable part of the land;

land; and it is said still to encroach and destroy more and more pasture; but I am not of opinion, that by any surveys or land-marks, its limits have been ever fixed, or its progression ascertained. If one man has confidence enough to say, that it advances, nobody can bring any proof to support him in denying it. The reason why it is not spread to a greater extent, seems to be, that the wind and rain come almost together, and that it is made close and heavy by the wet before the storms can put it in motion. So thick is the bed, and so small the particles, that if a traveller should be caught by a sudden gust in dry weather, he would find it very difficult to escape with life.

For natural curiosities, I was shown only two great masses of stone, which lie loose upon the ground; one on the top of a hill, and the other at a small distance from the bottom. They certainly were never put into their prefent places by human ftrength or fkill; and though an earthquake might have broken off the lower ftone, and rolled it into the valley, no account can be given of the other, which lies on the hill, unlefs, which I forgot to examine, there be ftill near it fome higher rock, from which it might be torn. All nations have a tradition, that their earlieft anceftors were giants, and thefe ftones are faid to have been thrown up and down by a giant and his miftrefs. There are fo many more important things, of which human knowledge can give no account, that it may be forgiven us, if we fpeculate no longer on two ftones in *Col*.

This Ifland is very populous. About nine-and-twenty years ago, the fencible men of *Col* were reckoned one hundred and forty, which is the fixth of eight hundred and forty; and probably fome contrived to be left out of the lift. The Minifter told us, that a few years ago the inhabitants were eight hundred, between the ages of seven and of seventy. Round numbers are seldom exact. But in this cafe the authority is good, and the errour likely to be little. If to the eight hundred be added what the laws of computation require, they will be increafed to at leaft a thoufand; and if the dimenfions of the country have been accurately related, every mile maintains more than twenty-five.

This proportion of habitation is greater than the appearance of the country feems to admit; for wherever the eye wanders, it feems much wafte and little cultivation. I am more inclined to extend the land, of which no meafure has ever been taken, than to diminifh the people, who have been really numbered. Let it be fuppofed, that a computed mile contains a mile and a half, as was commonly found true in the menfuration of the *Englifh* roads, and we fhall then

then allot nearly twelve to a mile, which agrees much better with ocular observation.

Here as in *Sky* and other Islands, are the Laird, the Tackſmen, and the under-tenants.

Mr. *Maclean*, the Laird, has very extenſive poſſeſſions, being proprietor, not only of far the greater part of *Col*, but of the extenſive Iſland of *Rum*, and a very conſiderable territory in *Mull*.

Rum is one of the larger Iſlands, almoſt ſquare, and therefore of great capacity in proportion to its ſides. By the uſual method of eſtimating computed extent, it may contain more than a hundred and twenty ſquare miles.

It originally belonged to *Clanronald*, and was purchaſed by *Col*; who, in ſome diſpute

pute about the bargain, made *Clanronald* prisoner, and kept him nine months in confinement. Its owner represents it as mountainous, rugged, and barren. In the hills there are red deer. The horses are very small, but of a breed eminent for beauty. *Col*, not long ago, bought one of them from a tenant; who told him, that as he was of a shape uncommonly elegant, he could not sell him but at a high price; and that whoever had him should pay a guinea and a half.

There are said to be in *Barra*, a race of horses yet smaller, of which the highest is not above thirty-six inches.

The rent of *Rum* is not great. Mr. *Maclean* declared, that he should be very rich if he could set his land at two pence halfpenny an acre. The inhabitants are fifty-eight families, who continued Papists for some time after the Laird became a Protestant.

testant. Their adherence to their old religion was strengthened by the countenance of the Laird's sister, a zealous Romanist, till one Sunday, as they were going to mass under the conduct of their patroness, *Maclean* met them on the way, gave one of them a blow on the head with a *yellow stick*, I suppose a cane, for which the *Earse* had no name, and drove them to the kirk, from which they have never since departed. Since the use of this method of conversion, the inhabitants of *Egg* and *Canna*, who continue Papists, call the Protestantism of *Rum*, the religion of the *Yellow Stick*.

The only Popish Islands are *Egg* and *Canna*. *Egg* is the principal Island of a parish, in which, though he has no congregation, the Protestant Minister resides. I have heard of nothing curious in it, but the cave in which a former generation of the Islanders were smothered by *Macleod*.

If we had travelled with more leisure, it had not been fit to have neglected the Popish Islands. Popery is favourable to ceremony; and among ignorant nations, ceremony is the only preservative of tradition. Since Protestantism was extended to the savage parts of Scotland, it has perhaps been one of the chief labours of the Ministers to abolish stated observances, because they continued the remembrance of the former religion. We therefore who came to hear old traditions, and see antiquated manners, should probably have found them amongst the Papists.

Canna, the other Popish Island, belongs to *Clanronald*. It is said not to comprise more than twelve miles of land, and yet maintains as many inhabitants as *Rum*.

We were at *Col* under the protection of the young Laird, without any of the distresses, which Mr. *Pennant*, in a fit of simple

ple credulity, seems to think almost worthy of an elegy by Ossian. Wherever we roved, we were pleased to see the reverence with which his subjects regarded him. He did not endeavour to dazzle them by any magnificence of dress: his only distinction was a feather in his bonnet; but as soon as he appeared, they forsook their work and clustered about him: he took them by the hand, and they seemed mutually delighted. He has the proper disposition of a Chieftain, and seems desirous to continue the customs of his house. The bagpiper played regularly, when dinner was served, whose person and dress made a good appearance; and he brought no disgrace upon the family of *Rankin*, which has long supplied the Lairds of *Col* with hereditary musick.

The Tacksmen of *Col* seem to live with less dignity and convenience than those of *Sky*; where they had good houses, and tables not only plentiful, but delicate. In

Col only two houses pay the window-tax; for only two have six windows, which, I suppose, are the Laird's and Mr. *Macsweyn*'s.

The rents have, till within seven years, been paid in kind, but the tenants finding that cattle and corn varied in their price, desired for the future to give their landlord money; which, not having yet arrived at the philosophy of commerce, they consider as being every year of the same value.

We were told of a particular mode of undertenure. The Tacksman admits some of his inferior neighbours to the cultivation of his grounds, on condition that performing all the work, and giving a third part of the seed, they shall keep a certain number of cows, sheep, and goats, and reap a third part of the harvest. Thus by less than the tillage of two acres they pay the rent of one.

There

There are tenants below the rank of Tackſmen, that have got ſmaller tenants under them; for in every place, where money is not the general equivalent, there muſt be ſome whoſe labour is immediately paid by daily food.

A country that has no money, is by no means convenient for beggars, both becauſe ſuch countries are commonly poor, and becauſe charity requires ſome trouble and ſome thought. A penny is eaſily given upon the firſt impulſe of compaſſion, or impatience of importunity; but few will deliberately ſearch their cupboards or their granaries to find out ſomething to give. A penny is likewiſe eaſily ſpent; but victuals, if they are unprepared, require houſeroom, and fire, and utenſils, which the beggar knows not where to find.

Yet beggars there ſometimes are, who wander from Iſland to Iſland. We had,

in

in our passage to *Mull*, the company of a woman and her child, who had exhausted the charity of *Col*. The arrival of a beggar on an Island is accounted a siniftrous event. Every body considers that he shall have the less for what he gives away. Their alms, I believe, is generally oatmeal.

Near to *Col* is another Island called *Tireye*, eminent for its fertility. Though it has but half the extent of *Rum*, it is so well peopled, that there have appeared, not long ago, nine hundred and fourteen at a funeral. The plenty of this Island enticed beggars to it, who seemed so burthensome to the inhabitants, that a formal compact was drawn up, by which they obliged themselves to grant no more relief to casual wanderers, because they had among them an indigent woman of high birth, whom they considered as entitled to all that they could spare. I have read the stipulation, which

which was indited with juridical formality, but was never made valid by regular subscription.

If the inhabitants of *Col* have nothing to give, it is not that they are oppressed by their landlord: their leases seem to be very profitable. One farmer, who pays only seven pounds a year, has maintained seven daughters and three sons, of whom the eldest is educated at *Aberdeen* for the ministry; and now, at every vacation, opens a school in *Col*.

Life is here, in some respects, improved beyond the condition of some other Islands. In *Sky* what is wanted can only be bought, as the arrival of some wandering pedlar may afford an opportunity; but in *Col* there is a standing shop, and in *Mull* there are two. A shop in the Islands, as in other places of little frequentation, is a repository of every thing requisite for common use. Mr. *Boswell's*

Boſwell's journal was filled, and he bought some paper in *Col*. To a man that ranges the streets of *London*, where he is tempted to contrive wants for the pleasure of supplying them, a shop affords no image worthy of attention; but in an Island, it turns the balance of existence between good and evil. To live in perpetual want of little things, is a state not indeed of torture, but of constant vexation. I have in *Sky* had some difficulty to find ink for a letter; and if a woman breaks her needle, the work is at a stop.

As it is, the Islanders are obliged to content themselves with succedaneous means for many common purposes. I have seen the chief man of a very wide district riding with a halter for a bridle, and governing his hobby with a wooden curb.

The people of *Col*, however, do not want dexterity to supply some of their necessities.

neceffities. Several arts which make trades, and demand apprenticefhips in great cities, are here the practices of daily economy. In every houfe candles are made, both moulded and dipped. Their wicks are fmall fhreds of linen cloth. They all know how to extract from the Cuddy, oil for their lamps. They all tan fkins, and make brogues.

As we travelled through *Sky*, we faw many cottages, but they very frequently ftood fingle on the naked ground. In *Col*, where the hills opened a place convenient for habitation, we found a petty village of which every hut had a little garden adjoining; thus they made an appearance of focial commerce and mutual offices, and of fome attention to convenience and future fupply. There is not in the *Weftern Iflands* any collection of buildings that can make pretenfions to be called a town, except in the Ifle of *Lewis*, which I have not feen.

If

If *Lewis* is distinguished by a town, *Col* has also something peculiar. The young Laird has attempted what no Islander perhaps ever thought on. He has begun a road capable of a wheel-carriage. He has carried it about a mile, and will continue it by annual elongation from his house to the harbour.

Of taxes here is no reason for complaining; they are paid by a very easy composition. The *malt-tax* for *Col* is twenty shillings. Whisky is very plentiful: there are several stills in the Island, and more is made than the inhabitants consume.

The great business of insular policy is now to keep the people in their own country. As the world has been let in upon them, they have heard of happier climates, and less arbitrary government; and if they are disgusted, have emissaries among them ready to offer them land and houses, as a
reward

reward for deserting their Chief and Clan. Many have departed both from the main of *Scotland*, and from the Islands; and all that go may be considered as subjects lost to the *British* crown; for a nation scattered in the boundless regions of *America* resembles rays diverging from a focus. All the rays remain, but the heat is gone. Their power consisted in their concentration: when they are dispersed they have no effect.

It may be thought that they are happier by the change; but they are not happy as a nation, for they are a nation no longer. As they contribute not to the prosperity of any community, they must want that security, that dignity, that happiness, whatever it be, which a prosperous community throws back upon individuals.

The inhabitants of *Col* have not yet learned to be weary of their heath and rocks,

rocks, but attend their agriculture and their dairies, without listening to American seducements.

There are some however who think that this emigration has raised terrour disproportionate to its real evil; and that it is only a new mode of doing what was always done. The Highlands, they say, never maintained their natural inhabitants; but the people, when they found themselves too numerous, instead of extending cultivation, provided for themselves by a more compendious method, and sought better fortune in other countries. They did not indeed go away in collective bodies, but withdrew invisibly, a few at a time; but the whole number of fugitives was not less, and the difference between other times and this, is only the same as between evaporation and effusion.

This is plausible, but I am afraid it is not true. Those who went before, if they
were

were not sensibly missed, as the argument supposes, must have gone either in less number, or in a manner less detrimental, than at present; because formerly there was no complaint. Those who then left the country were generally the idle dependants on overburdened families, or men who had no property; and therefore carried away only themselves. In the present eagerness of emigration, families, and almost communities, go away together. Those who were considered as prosperous and wealthy sell their stock and carry away the money. Once none went away but the useless and poor; in some parts there is now reason to fear, that none will stay but those who are too poor to remove themselves, and too useless to be removed at the cost of others.

Of antiquity there is not more knowledge in *Col* than in other places; but every where something may be gleaned.

How ladies were portioned, when there was no money, it would be difficult for an *Englishman* to guess. In 1649, *Maclean* of *Dronart* in *Mull* married his sister *Fingala* to *Maclean* of *Col*, with a hundred and eighty kine; and stipulated, that if she became a widow, her jointure should be three hundred and sixty. I suppose some proportionate tract of land was appropriated to their pasturage.

The disposition to pompous and expensive funerals, which has at one time or other prevailed in most parts of the civilized world, is not yet suppressed in the Islands, though some of the ancient solemnities are worn away, and singers are no longer hired to attend the procession. Nineteen years ago, at the burial of the Laird of *Col*, were killed thirty cows, and about fifty sheep. The number of the cows is positively told, and we must suppose other victuals in like proportion.

Mr.

Mr. *Maclean* informed us of an odd game, of which he did not tell the original, but which may perhaps be used in other places, where the reason of it is not yet forgot. At New-year's eve, in the hall or castle of the Laird, where, at festal seasons, there may be supposed a very numerous company, one man dresses himself in a cow's hide, upon which other men beat with sticks. He runs with all this noise round the house, which all the company quits in a counterfeited fright: the door is then shut. At New-year's eve there is no great pleasure to be had out of doors in the *Hebrides*. They are sure soon to recover from their terrour enough to solicit for re-admission; which, for the honour of poetry, is not to be obtained but by repeating a verse, with which those that are knowing and provident take care to be furnished.

Very near the house of *Maclean* stands the castle of *Col*, which was the mansion of the Laird, till the house was built. It is built upon a rock, as Mr. *Boswell* remarked, that it might not be mined. It is very strong, and having been not long uninhabited, is yet in repair. On the wall was, not long ago, a stone with an inscription, importing, that *if any man of the Clan of Maclonich shall appear before this castle, though he come at midnight, with a man's head in his hand, he shall there find safety and protection against all but the King.*

This is an old Highland treaty made upon a very memorable occasion. *Maclean*, the son of *John Gerves*, who recovered *Col*, and conquered *Barra*, had obtained, it is said, from *James* the Second, a grant of the lands of *Lochiel*, forfeited, I suppose, by some offence against the state.

Forfeited estates were not in those days quietly resigned; *Maclean*, therefore, went with an armed force to seize his new possessions, and, I know not for what reason, took his wife with him. The *Camerons* rose in defence of their Chief, and a battle was fought at the head of *Loch Ness*, near the place where *Fort Augustus* now stands, in which *Lochiel* obtained the victory, and *Maclean*, with his followers, was defeated and destroyed.

The lady fell into the hands of the conquerors, and being found pregnant, was placed in the custody of *Maclonich*, one of a tribe or family branched from *Cameron*, with orders, if she brought a boy, to destroy him, if a girl, to spare her.

Maclonich's wife, who was with child likewise, had a girl about the same time at which lady *Maclean* brought a boy, and *Maclonich* with more generosity to his captive,

tive, than fidelity to his truft, contrived that the children fhould be changed.

Maclean being thus preferved from death, in time recovered his original patrimony; and in gratitude to his friend, made his caftle a place of refuge to any of the Clan that fhould think himfelf in danger; and as a proof of reciprocal confidence, *Maclean* took upon himfelf and his pofterity the care of educating the heir of *Maclonich*.

This ftory, like all other traditions of the Highlands, is varioufly related; but though fome circumftances are uncertain, the principal fact is true. *Maclean* undoubtedly owed his prefervation to *Maclonich*; for the treaty between the two families has been ftrictly obferved: it did not fink into difufe and oblivion, but continued in its full force while the chieftains retained their power. I have read a demand of protection, made not more than thirty-feven years

years ago, for one of the *Maclonichs*, named *Ewen Cameron*, who had been acceſſory to the death of *Macmartin*, and had been baniſhed by *Lochiel*, his lord, for a certain term; at the expiration of which he returned married from *France*; but the *Macmartins*, not ſatisfied with the puniſhment, when he attempted to ſettle, ſtill threatened him with vengeance. He therefore aſked, and obtained ſhelter in the Iſle of *Col*.

The power of protection ſubſiſts no longer; but what the law permits is yet continued, and *Maclean* of *Col* now educates the heir of *Maclonich*.

There ſtill remains in the Iſlands, though it is paſſing faſt away, the cuſtom of foſterage. A Laird, a man of wealth and eminence, ſends his child, either male or female, to a tackſman, or tenant, to be foſtered. It is not always his own tenant, but ſome diſtant

distant friend that obtains this honour; for an honour such a trust is very reasonably thought. The terms of fosterage seem to vary in different islands. In *Mull* the father sends with his child a certain number of cows, to which the same number is added by the fosterer. The father appropriates a proportionable extent of ground, without rent, for their pasturage. If every cow brings a calf, half belongs to the fosterer, and half to the child; but if there be only one calf between two cows, it is the child's, and when the child returns to the parents, it is accompanied by all the cows given, both by the father and by the fosterer, with half of the increase of the flock by propagation. These beasts are considered as a portion, and called *Macalive* cattle, of which the father has the produce, but is supposed not to have the full property, but to owe the same number to the child, as a portion to the daughter, or a stock for the son.

Children continue with the fosterer perhaps six years, and cannot, where this is the practice, be considered as burdensome. The fosterer, if he gives four cows, receives likewise four, and has, while the child continues with him, grass for eight without rent, with half the calves, and all the milk, for which he pays only four cows when he dismisses his *Dalt*, for that is the name for a foster child.

Fosterage is, I believe, sometimes performed upon more liberal terms. Our friend, the young Laird of *Col*, was fostered by *Macsweyn* of *Grissipol*. *Macsweyn* then lived a tenant to Sir *James Macdonald* in the Isle of *Sky*: and therefore *Col*, whether he sent him cattle or not, could grant him no land. The *Dalt*, however, at his return, brought back a considerable number of *Macalive cattle*, and of the friendship so formed there have been good effects. When *Macdonald* raised his rents,

rents, *Macfweyn* was, like other tenants, discontented, and, resigning his farm, removed from *Sky* to *Col*, and was established at *Griffipol*.

These observations we made by favour of the contrary wind that drove us to *Col*, an Island not often visited; for there is not much to amuse curiosity, or to attract avarice.

The ground has been hitherto, I believe, used chiefly for pasturage. In a district, such as the eye can command, there is a general herdsman, who knows all the cattle of the neighbourhood, and whose station is upon a hill, from which he surveys the lower grounds; and if one man's cattle invade another's grass, drives them back to their own borders. But other means of profit begin to be found; kelp is gathered and burnt, and sloops are loaded with the concreted ashes. Cultivation is likely to be improved by the skill and encouragement

couragement of the prefent heir, and the inhabitants of thofe obfcure vallies will partake of the general progrefs of life.

The rents of the parts which belong to the Duke of Argyle, have been raifed from fifty-five to one hundred and five pounds, whether from the land or the fea I cannot tell. The bounties of the fea have lately been fo great, that a farm in Southuift has rifen in ten years from a rent of thirty pounds to one hundred and eighty.

He who lives in *Col,* and finds himfelf condemned to folitary meals, and incommunicable reflection, will find the ufefulnefs of that middle order of Tackfmen, which, fome who applaud their own wifdom are wifhing to deftroy. Without intelligence man is not focial, he is only gregarious; and little intelligence will there be, where all are conftrained to daily labour, and every mind muft wait upon the hand.

After having listened for some days to the tempest, and wandered about the Island till our curiosity was satisfied, we began to think about our departure. To leave *Col* in October was not very easy. We however found a sloop which lay on the coast to carry kelp; and for a price which we thought levied upon our necessities, the master agreed to carry us to *Mull*, whence we might readily pass back to *Scotland*.

MULL.

As we were to catch the first favourable breath, we spent the night not very elegantly nor pleasantly in the vessel, and were landed next day at *Tobor Morar*, a port in *Mull*, which appears to an unexperienced eye formed for the security of ships; for its mouth is closed by a small island; which admits them through narrow channels into a bason sufficiently capacious. They are indeed safe from the sea, but there

there is a hollow between the mountains, through which the wind iffues from the land with very mifchievous violence.

There was no danger while we were there, and we found feveral other veffels at anchor; fo that the port had a very commercial appearance.

The young Laird of *Col*, who had determined not to let us lofe his company, while there was any difficulty remaining, came over with us. His influence foon appeared; for he procured us horfes, and conducted us to the houfe of Doctor *Macclean*, where we found very kind entertainment, and very pleafing converfation. Mifs *Maclean*, who was born, and had been bred at *Glafgow*, having removed with her father to *Mull*, added to other qualifications, a great knowledge of the *Earfe* language, which fhe had not learned in her childhood, but gained by ftudy, and was the only interpreter of *Earse* poetry that I could ever find.

The Isle of *Mull* is perhaps in extent the third of the *Hebrides*. It is not broken by waters, nor shot into promontories, but is a solid and compact mass, of breadth nearly equal to its length. Of the dimensions of the larger Islands, there is no knowledge approaching to exactness. I am willing to estimate it as containing about three hundred square miles.

Mull had suffered like *Sky* by the black winter of seventy-one, in which, contrary to all experience, a continued frost detained the snow eight weeks upon the ground. Against a calamity never known, no provision had been made, and the people could only pine in helpless misery. One tenant was mentioned, whose cattle perished to the value of three hundred pounds; a loss which probably more than the life of man is necessary to repair. In countries like these, the descriptions of famine become intelligible. Where by vigorous and artful cultivation of a soil naturally fertile, there is commonly a superfluous growth both of grain and grass; where the fields are crowded with cattle; and where every hand is able to attract wealth from a distance, by making something that promotes ease, or gratifies vanity, a dear year produces only a comparative want, which is rather seen than felt, and which terminates commonly in no worse effect, than that of condemning the lower orders of the community to sacrifice a little luxury to convenience, or at most a little convenience to necessity.

But where the climate is unkind, and the ground penurious, so that the most fruitful years produce only enough to maintain themselves; where life unimproved, and unadorned, fades into something little more than naked exiſtence, and every one is buſy for himſelf, without any arts by which the pleaſure of others may be increaſed; if to the daily burden of diſtreſs any additional weight be added, nothing remains but to deſpair and die. In *Mull* the diſappointment of a harveſt, or a murrain among the cattle, cuts off the regular proviſion; and they who have no manufactures can purchaſe no part of the ſuperfluities of other countries. The conſequence of a bad ſeaſon is here not ſcarcity, but emptineſs; and they whoſe plenty was barely a ſupply of natural and preſent need, when that ſlender ſtock fails, muſt periſh with hunger.

All travel has its advantages. If the paſſenger viſits better countries, he may learn to improve his own, and if fortune carries him to worſe, he may learn to enjoy it.

Mr. *Boſwell*'s curioſity ſtrongly impelled him to ſurvey *Iona*, or *Icolmkill*, which was

to

to the early ages the great school of Theology, and is supposed to have been the place of sepulture for the ancient kings. I, though less eager, did not oppose him.

That we might perform this expedition, it was necessary to traverse a great part of *Mull.* We passed a day at Dr. *Maclean*'s, and could have been well contented to stay longer. But *Col* provided us horses, and we pursued our journey. This was a day of inconvenience, for the country is very rough, and my horse was but little. We travelled many hours through a tract, black and barren, in which, however, there were the reliques of humanity; for we found a ruined chapel in our way.

It is natural, in traversing this gloom of desolation, to inquire, whether something may not be done to give Nature a more cheerful face, and whether those hills and moors that afford heath cannot with a little care and labour bear something better? The first thought that occurs is to cover them with trees, for that in many of these naked regions trees will grow, is evident, because stumps and roots are yet remaining; and the speculatist hastily proceeds to censure that negligence and laziness that has omitted for so long a time so easy an improvement.

To drop seeds into the ground, and attend their growth, requires little labour and no skill. He who remembers that all the woods, by which the wants of man have been supplied from the Deluge till now, were self-sown, will not easily be persuaded to think all the art and preparation necessary which the Georgick writers prescribe to planters. Trees certainly have covered the earth with very little culture. They wave their tops among the rocks of *Norway*, and might thrive as well in the Highlands and *Hebrides*.

But

But there is a frightful interval between the feed and timber. He that calculates the growth of trees, has the unwelcome remembrance of the shortness of life driven hard upon him. He knows that he is doing what will never benefit himself; and when he rejoices to see the stem rise, is disposed to repine that another shall cut it down.

Plantation is naturally the employment of a mind unburdened with care, and vacant to futurity, saturated with present good, and at leisure to derive gratification from the prospect of posterity. He that pines with hunger, is in little care how others shall be fed. The poor man is seldom studious to make his grandson rich. It may be soon discovered, why in a place, which hardly supplies the cravings of necessity, there has been little attention to the delights of fancy, and why distant convenience is unregarded, where the thoughts are turned with inceffant folicitude upon every poffibility of immediate advantage.

Neither is it quite fo eafy to raife large woods, as may be conceived. Trees intended to produce timber muft be fown where they are to grow; and ground fown with trees muft be kept ufelefs for a long time, inclofed at an expence from which many will be difcouraged by the remotenefs of the profit, and watched with that attention, which, in places where it is moft needed, will neither be given nor bought. That it cannot be plowed is evident; and if cattle be fuffered to graze upon it, they will devour the plants as faft as they rife. Even in coarfer countries, where herds and flocks are not fed, not only the deer and the wild goats will browfe upon them, but the hare and rabbit will nibble them. It is therefore reafonable to believe, what I do not remember any naturalift to have remarked, that there was a time when the world was

very

very thinly inhabited by beafts, as well as men, and that the woods had leifure to rife high before animals had bred numbers fufficient to intercept them.

Sir *James Macdonald*, in part of the waftes of his territory, fet or fowed trees, to the number, as I have been told, of feveral millions, expecting, doubtlefs, that they would grow up into future navies and cities; but for want of inclofure, and of that care which is always neceffary, and will hardly ever be taken, all his coft and labour have been loft, and the ground is likely to continue an ufelefs heath.

Having not any experience of a journey in *Mull*, we had no doubt of reaching the fea by day-light, and therefore had not left Dr. *Maclean*'s very early. We travelled diligently enough, but found the country, for road there was none, very difficult to pafs. We were always ftruggling with
fome

some obstruction or other, and our vexation was not balanced by any gratification of the eye or mind. We were now long enough acquainted with hills and heath to have lost the emotion that they once raised, whether pleasing or painful, and had our mind employed only on our own fatigue. We were however sure, under *Col*'s protection, of escaping all real evils. There was no house in *Mull* to which he could not introduce us. He had intended to lodge us, for that night, with a gentleman that lived upon the coast, but discovered on the way, that he then lay in bed without hope of life.

We resolved not to embarrass a family, in a time of so much sorrow, if any other expedient could be found; and as the Island of *Ulva* was over-against us, it was determined that we should pass the strait and have recourse to the Laird, who, like the other gentlemen of the Islands, was known

to

to *Col*. We expected to find a ferry-boat, but when at last we came to the water, the boat was gone.

We were now again at a stop. It was the sixteenth of October, a time when it is not convenient to sleep in the *Hebrides* without a cover, and there was no house within our reach, but that which we had already declined.

U L V A.

While we stood deliberating, we were happily espied from an *Irish* ship, that lay at anchor in the strait. The master saw that we wanted a passage, and with great civility sent us his boat, which quickly conveyed us to *Ulva*, where we were very liberally entertained by Mr. *Macquarry*.

To *Ulva* we came in the dark, and left it before noon the next day. A very exact description

description therefore will not be expected. We were told, that it is an Island of no great extent, rough and barren, inhabited by the *Macquarrys*; a Clan not powerful nor numerous, but of antiquity, which most other families are content to reverence. The name is supposed to be a depravation of some other; for the *Earse* language does not afford it any etymology. *Macquarry* is proprietor both of *Ulva* and some adjacent Islands, among which is *Staffa*, so lately raised to renown by Mr. *Banks*.

When the Islanders were reproached with their ignorance, or insensibility of the wonders of *Staffa*, they had not much to reply. They had indeed considered it little, because they had always seen it; and none but philosophers, nor they always, are struck with wonder, otherwise than by novelty. How would it surprise an unenlightened ploughman, to hear a company of sober men, inquiring by what power the hand tosses a stone, or why the stone, when it is tossed, falls to the ground!

Of the ancestors of *Macquarry*, who thus lies hid in his unfrequented Island, I have found memorials in all places where they could be expected.

Inquiring after the reliques of former manners, I found that in *Ulva*, and, I think, no where else, is continued the payment of the *Mercheta Mulierum*; a fine in old times due to the Laird at the marriage of a virgin. The original of this claim, as of our tenure of *Borough English*, is variously delivered. It is pleasant to find ancient customs in old families. This payment, like others, was, for want of money, made anciently in the produce of the land. *Macquarry* was used to demand a sheep, for which he now takes a crown, by that inattention to the uncertain proportion between

tween the value and the denomination of money, which has brought much diforder into *Europe*. A sheep has always the same power of supplying human wants, but a crown will bring at one time more, at another less.

Ulva was not neglected by the piety of ancient times: it has still to show what was once a church.

INCH KENNETH:

In the morning we went again into the boat, and were landed on *Inch Kenneth*, an Island about a mile long, and perhaps half a mile broad, remarkable for pleasantness and fertility. It is verdant and grassy, and fit both for pasture and tillage; but it has no trees. Its only inhabitants were Sir *Allan Maclean*, and two young ladies, his daughters, with their servants.

Romance

Romance does not often exhibit a scene that strikes the imagination more than this little desert in these depths of Western obscurity, occupied not by a gross herdsman, or amphibious fisherman, but by a gentleman and two ladies, of high birth, polished manners, and elegant conversation, who, in a habitation raised not very far above the ground, but furnished with unexpected neatness and convenience, practised all the kindness of hospitality, and refinement of courtesy.

Sir *Allan* is the Chieftain of the great Clan of *Maclean,* which is said to claim the second place among the Highland families, yielding only to *Macdonald.* Though by the misconduct of his ancestors, most of the extensive territory, which would have descended to him, has been alienated, he still retains much of the dignity and authority of his birth. When soldiers were lately wanting for the *American* war, application

was

was made to Sir *Allan*, and he nominated a hundred men for the service, who obeyed the summons, and bore arms under his command.

He had then, for some time, resided with the young ladies in *Inch Kenneth*, where he lives not only with plenty, but with elegance, having conveyed to his cottage a collection of books, and what else is necessary to make his hours pleasant.

When we landed, we were met by Sir *Allan* and the ladies, accompanied by Miss *Macquarry*, who had passed some time with them, and now returned to *Ulva* with her father.

We all walked together to the mansion, where we found one cottage for Sir *Allan*, and I think two more for the domesticks and the offices. We entered, and wanted little that palaces afford. Our room was neatly

neatly floored, and well lighted; and our dinner, which was dreffed in one of the other huts, was plentiful and delicate.

In the afternoon Sir *Allan* reminded us, that the day was Sunday, which he never fuffered to pafs without fome religious diftinction, and invited us to partake in his acts of domeftick worfhip; which I hope neither Mr. *Bofwell* nor myfelf will be fufpected of a difpofition to refufe. The elder of the ladies read the *Englifh* fervice.

Inch Kenneth was once a feminary of ecclefiafticks, fubordinate, I fuppofe, to *Icolmkill*. Sir *Allan* had a mind to trace the foundation of the college, but neither I nor Mr. *Bofwell*, who *bends* a keener *eye on vacancy*, were able to perceive them.

Our attention, however, was fufficiently engaged by a venerable chapel, which ftands yet entire, except that the roof is gone.

gone. It is about sixty feet in length, and thirty in breadth. On one side of the altar is a bas relief of the blessed Virgin, and by it lies a little bell; which, though cracked, and without a clapper, has remained there for ages, guarded only by the venerableness of the place. The ground round the chapel is covered with grave-stones of Chiefs and ladies; and still continues to be a place of sepulture.

Inch Kenneth is a proper prelude to *Icolmkill*. It was not without some mournful emotion that we contemplated the ruins of religious structures, and the monuments of the dead.

On the next day we took a more distinct view of the place, and went with the boat to see oysters in the bed, out of which the boat-men forced up as many as were wanted. Even *Inch Kenneth* has a subordinate Island, named *Sandiland*, I suppose,

in

in contempt, where we landed, and found a rock, with a surface of perhaps four acres, of which one is naked stone, another spread with sand and shells, some of which I picked up for their glossy beauty, and two covered with a little earth and grass, on which Sir *Allan* has a few sheep. I doubt not but when there was a college at *Inch Kenneth*, there was a hermitage upon *Sandiland*.

Having wandered over those extensive plains, we committed ourselves again to the winds and waters; and after a voyage of about ten minutes, in which we met with nothing very observable, were again safe upon dry ground.

We told Sir *Allan* our desire of visiting *Icolmkill*, and entreated him to give up his protection, and his company. He thought proper to hesitate a little; but the Ladies hinted, that as they knew he would not

finally

finally refuse, he would do better if he preserved the grace of ready compliance. He took their advice, and promised to carry us on the morrow in his boat.

We passed the remaining part of the day in such amusements as were in our power. Sir *Allan* related the *American* campaign, and at evening one of the Ladies played on her harpsichord, while *Col* and Mr. *Boswell* danced a *Scottish* reel with the other.

We could have been easily persuaded to a longer stay upon *Inch Kenneth*, but life will not be all passed in delight. The session at *Edinburgh* was approaching, from which Mr. *Boswell* could not be absent.

In the morning our boat was ready: it was high and strong. Sir *Allan* victualled it for the day, and provided able rowers. We now parted from the young Laird of *Col*, who had treated us with so much kindness, nefs, and concluded his favours by configning us to Sir *Allan*. Here we had the laſt embrace of this amiable man, who, while these pages were preparing to atteſt his virtues, perished in the paſſage between *Ulva* and *Inch Kenneth*.

Sir *Allan*, to whom the whole region was well known, told us of a very remarkable cave, to which he would show us the way. We had been difappointed already by one cave, and were not much elevated by the expectation of another.

It was yet better to fee it, and we ſtopped at fome rocks on the coaſt of *Mull*. The mouth is fortified by vaſt fragments of ſtone, over which we made our way, neither very nimbly, nor very fecurely. The place, however, well repaid our trouble. The bottom, as far as the flood ruſhes in, was encumbered with large pebbles, but as we advanced was spread over with smooth sand. The breadth is about forty-five feet: the roof rises in an arch, almost regular, to a height which we could not measure; but I think it about thirty feet.

This part of our curiosity was nearly frustrated; for though we went to see a cave, and knew that caves are dark, we forgot to carry tapers, and did not discover our omission till we were wakened by our wants. Sir *Allan* then sent one of the boatmen into the country, who soon returned with one little candle. We were thus enabled to go forward, but could not venture far. Having passed inward from the sea to a great depth, we found on the right hand a narrow passage, perhaps not more than six feet wide, obstructed by great stones, over which we climbed and came into a second cave, in breadth twenty-five feet. The air in this apartment was very warm, but not oppressive, nor loaded with vapours.

Our

Our light shewed no tokens of a feculent or corrupted atmosphere. Here was a square stone, called, as we are told, *Fingal's Table*.

If we had been provided with torches, we should have proceeded in our search, though we had already gone as far as any former adventurer, except some who are reported never to have returned; and, measuring our way back, we found it more than a hundred and sixty yards, the eleventh part of a mile.

Our measures were not critically exact, having been made with a walking pole, such as it is convenient to carry in these rocky countries, of which I guessed the length by standing against it. In this there could be no great errour, nor do I much doubt but the Highlander, whom we employed, reported the number right. More nicety however is better, and no man should travel unprovided with inſtruments for taking heights and diſtances.

There is yet another cauſe of errour not always eaſily ſurmounted, though more dangerous to the veracity of itinerary narratives, than imperfect menſuration. An obſerver deeply impreſſed by any remarkable ſpectacle, does not ſuppoſe, that the traces will ſoon vaniſh from his mind, and having commonly no great convenience for writing, defers the deſcription to a time of more leiſure, and better accommodation.

He who has not made the experiment, or who is not accuſtomed to require rigorous accuracy from himſelf, will ſcarcely believe how much a few hours take from certainty of knowledge, and diſtinctneſs of imagery; how the ſucceſſion of objects will be broken, how ſeparate parts will be confuſed, and how many particular features

and

and discriminations will be compressed and conglobated into one gross and general idea.

To this dilatory notation must be imputed the false relations of travellers, where there is no imaginable motive to deceive. They trusted to memory what cannot be trusted safely but to the eye, and told by guess what a few hours before they had known with certainty. Thus it was that *Wheeler* and *Spon* described with irreconcilable contrariety things which they surveyed together, and which both undoubtedly designed to show as they saw them.

When we had satisfied our curiosity in the cave, so far as our penury of light permitted us, we clambered again to our boats, and proceeded along the coast of *Mull* to a headland, called *Atun*, remarkable for the columnar form of the rocks, which rise in a series of pilasters, with a degree of regularity, which Sir *Allan* thinks not less worthy of curiosity than the shore of *Staffa*.

Not long after we came to another range of black rocks, which had the appearance of broken pilasters, set one behind another to a great depth. - This place was chosen by Sir *Allan* for our dinner. We were easily accommodated with seats, for the stones were of all heights, and refreshed ourselves and our boatmen, who could have no other rest till we were at *Icolmkill*.

The evening was now approaching, and we were yet at a considerable distance from the end of our expedition. We could therefore stop no more to make remarks in the way, but set forward with some degree of of eagerneſs. The day ſoon failed us, and the moon preſented a very ſolemn and pleaſing ſcene. The ſky was clear, ſo that the eye commanded a wide circle: the ſea was neither ſtill nor turbulent: the wind neither ſilent nor loud. We were never far from one coaſt or another, on which, if the weather had become violent, we could have found ſhelter, and therefore contemplated at eaſe the region through which we glided in the tranquillity of the night, and ſaw now a rock and now an iſland grow gradually conſpicuous and gradually obſcure. I committed the fault which I have juſt been cenſuring, in neglecting, as we paſſed, to note the ſeries of this placid navigation.

We were very near an Iſland, called *Nun's Iſland*, perhaps from an ancient convent. Here is ſaid to have been dug the ſtone which was uſed in the buildings of
Icolmkill.

Icolmkill. Whether it is now inhabited we could not stay to inquire.

At last we came to *Icolmkill*, but found no convenience for landing. Our boat could not be forced very near the dry ground, and our Highlanders carried us over the water.

We were now treading that illustrious Island, which was once the luminary of the *Caledonian* regions, whence savage Clans and roving barbarians derived the benefits of knowledge, and the blessings of religion. To abstract the mind from all local emotion would be impossible, if it were endeavoured, and would be foolish, if it were possible. Whatever withdraws us from the power of our senses; whatever makes the past, the distant, or the future predominate over the present, advances us in the dignity of thinking beings. Far from me and from my friends,

friends, be such frigid philosophy as may conduct us indifferent and unmoved over any ground which has been dignified by wisdom, bravery, or virtue. That man is little to be envied, whose patriotism would not gain force upon the plain of *Marathon*, or whose piety would not grow warmer among the ruins of *Iona*.

We came too late to visit monuments: some care was necessary for ourselves. Whatever was in the Island, Sir *Allan* could demand, for the inhabitants were *Macleans*; but having little they could not give us much. He went to the headman of the Island, whom Fame, but Fame delights in amplifying, represents as worth no less than fifty pounds. He was perhaps, proud enough of his guests, but ill prepared for our entertainment; however, he soon produced more provision than men not luxurious require. Our lodging was next to be provided. We found a barn well
stocked

stocked with hay, and made our beds as soft as we could.

In the morning we rose and surveyed the place. The churches of the two convents are both standing, though unroofed. They were built of unhewn stone, but solid, and not inelegant. I brought away rude measures of the buildings, such as I cannot much trust myself, inaccurately taken, and obscurely noted. Mr. *Pennant*'s delineations, which are doubtless exact, have made my unskilful description less necessary.

The episcopal church consists of two parts, separated by the belfry, and built at different times. The original church had, like others, the altar at one end, and tower at the other; but as it grew too small, another building of equal dimension was added, and the tower then was necessarily in the middle.

That

That these edifices are of different ages seems evident. The arch of the first church is *Roman*, being part of a circle; that of the additional building is pointed, and therefore *Gothick*, or *Saracenical*; the tower is firm, and wants only to be floored and covered.

Of the chambers or cells belonging to the monks, there are some walls remaining, but nothing approaching to a complete apartment.

The bottom of the church is so incumbered with mud and rubbish, that we could make no discoveries of curious inscriptions, and what there are have been already published. The place is said to be known where the black stones lie concealed, on which the old Highland Chiefs, when they made contracts and alliances, used to take the oath, which was considered as more sacred than any other obligation, and which

could

could not be violated without the blackest infamy. In those days of violence and rapine, it was of great importance to impress upon savage minds the sanctity of an oath, by some particular and extraordinary circumstances. They would not have recourse to the black stones, upon small or common occasions, and when they had established their faith by this tremendous sanction, inconstancy and treachery were no longer feared.

The chapel of the nunnery is now used by the inhabitants as a kind of general cow-house, and the bottom is consequently too miry for examination. Some of the stones which covered the later abbesses have inscriptions, which might yet be read, if the chapel were cleansed. The roof of this, as of all the other buildings, is totally destroyed, not only because timber quickly decays when it is neglected, but because in an island utterly destitute of wood,

it

it was wanted for use, and was consequently the first plunder of needy rapacity.

The chancel of the nuns' chapel is covered with an arch of stone, to which time has done no injury; and a small apartment communicating with the choir, on the north side, like the chapter-house in cathedrals, roofed with stone in the same manner, is likewise entire.

In one of the churches was a marble altar, which the superstition of the inhabitants has destroyed. Their opinion was, that a fragment of this stone was a defence against shipwrecks, fire, and miscarriages. In one corner of the church the bason for holy water is yet unbroken.

The cemetry of the nunnery was, till very lately, regarded with such reverence, that only women were buried in it. These reliques of veneration always produce some
mournful

mournful pleasure. I could have forgiven a great injury more easily than the violation of this imaginary sanctity.

South of the chapel stand the walls of a large room, which was probably the hall, or refectory of the nunnery. This apartment is capable of repair. Of the rest of the convent there are only fragments.

Besides the two principal churches, there are, I think, five chapels yet standing, and three more remembered. There are also crosses, of which two bear the names of St. *John* and St. *Matthew*.

A large space of ground about these consecrated edifices is covered with gravestones, few of which have any inscription. He that surveys it, attended by an insular antiquary, may be told where the Kings of many nations are buried, and if he loves to sooth his imagination with the thoughts

thoughts that naturally rife in places where the great and the powerful lie mingled with the duft, let him liften in fubmiffive filence; for if he afks any queftions, his delight is at an end.

Iona has long enjoyed, without any very credible atteftation, the honour of being reputed the cemetery of the *Scottiſh* Kings. It is not unlikely, that, when the opinion of local fanctity was prevalent, the Chieftains of the Ifles, and perhaps fome of the *Norwegian* or *Iriſh* princes, were repofited in this venerable enclofure. But by whom the fubterraneous vaults are peopled is now utterly unknown. The graves are very numerous, and fome of them undoubtedly contain the remains of men, who did not expect to be fo foon forgotten.

Not far from this awful ground, may be traced the garden of the monaftery: the fiſhponds are yet difcernible, and the aqueduct,

aqueduct, which supplied them, is still in use.

There remains a broken building, which is called the Bishop's house, I know not by what authority. It was once the residence of some man above the common rank, for it has two stories and a chimney. We were shewn a chimney at the other end, which was only a nich, without perforation, but so much does antiquarian credulity, or patriotick vanity prevail, that it was not much more safe to trust the eye of our instructor than the memory.

There is in the Island one house more, and only one, that has a chimney; we entered it, and found it neither wanting repair nor inhabitants; but to the farmers, who now possess it, the chimney is of no great value; for their fire was made on the floor, in the middle of the room, and notwithstanding the dignity of their mansion, they

they rejoiced, like their neighbours, in the comforts of smoke.

It is observed, that ecclesiastical colleges are always in the most pleasant and fruitful places. While the world allowed the monks their choice, it is surely no dishonour that they chose well. This Island is remarkably fruitful. The village near the churches is said to contain seventy families, which, at five in a family, is more than a hundred inhabitants to a mile. There are perhaps other villages; yet both corn and cattle are annually exported.

But the fruitfulness of *Iona* is now its whole prosperity. The inhabitants are remarkably gross, and remarkably neglected: I know not if they are visited by any Minister. The Island, which was once the metropolis of learning and piety, has now no school for education, nor temple for worship, only two inhabitants that can speak *English*, and not one that can write or read.

The people are of the Clan of *Maclean*; and though Sir *Allan* had not been in the place for many years, he was received with all the reverence due to their Chieftain. One of them being sharply reprehended by him, for not sending him some rum, declared after his departure, in Mr. *Boswell*'s presence, that he had no design of disappointing him, *for*, said he, *I would cut my bones for him*; and if he had sent his dog for it, he should have had it.

When we were to depart, our boat was left by the ebb at a great distance from the water, but no sooner did we wish it afloat, than the islanders gathered round it, and, by the union of many hands, pushed it down the beach; every man who could contribute his help feemed to think himfelf happy in the opportunity of being, for a moment, ufeful to his Chief.

We now left thofe illuftrious ruins, by which Mr. *Bofwell* was much affected, nor would I willingly be thought to have looked upon them without fome emotion. Perhaps, in the revolutions of the world, *Iona* may be fometime again the inftructrefs of the Weftern Regions.

It was no long voyage to *Mull*, where, under Sir *Allan*'s protection, we landed in the evening, and were entertained for the night by Mr. *Maclean*, a Minifter that lives upon the coaft, whofe elegance of converfation, and ftrength of judgment, would make him confpicuous in places of greater celebrity. Next day we dined with Dr. *Maclean*, another phyfician, and then travelled on to the houfe of a very powerful Laird,

Laird, *Maclean* of *Lochbuy*; for in this country every man's name is *Maclean*.

Where races are thus numerous, and thus combined, none but the Chief of a clan is addressed by his name. The Laird of *Dunvegan* is called *Macleod*, but other gentlemen of the same family are denominated by the places where they reside, as *Raasa*, or *Talisker*. The distinction of the meaner people is made by their Christian names. In consequence of this practice, the late Laird of *Macfarlane*, an eminent genealogist, considered himself as disrespectfully treated, if the common addition was applied to him. Mr. *Macfarlane*, said he, may with equal propriety be said to many; but I, and I only, am *Macfarlane*.

Our afternoon journey was through a country of such gloomy desolation, that Mr. *Boswell* thought no part of the Highlands equally terrifick, yet we came without

out any difficulty, at evening, to *Lochbuy*, where we found a true Highland Laird, rough and haughty, and tenacious of his dignity; who, hearing my name, inquired whether I was of the *Johnstons of Glencoe*, or of *Ardnamurchan?*

Lochbuy has, like the other insular Chieftains, quitted the castle that sheltered his ancestors, and lives near it, in a mansion not very spacious or splendid. I have seen no houses in the Islands much to be envied for convenience or magnificence, yet they bear testimony to the progress of arts and civility, as they shew that rapine and surprise are no longer dreaded, and are much more commodious than the ancient fortresses.

The castles of the *Hebrides*, many of which are standing, and many ruined, were always built upon points of land, on the margin of the sea. For the choice of this fituation there muft have been, fome general reafon, which the change of manners has left in obfcurity. They were of no ufe in the days of piracy, as defences of the coaft; for it was equally acceffible in other places. Had they been fea-marks or light-houfes, they would have been of more ufe to the invader than the natives, who could want no fuch directions on their own waters: for a watch-tower, a cottage on a hill would have been better, as it would have commanded a wider view.

If they be confidered merely as places of retreat, the fituation feems not well chofen; for the Laird of an Ifland is fafeft from foreign enemies in the centre: on the coaft he might be more fuddenly furprifed than in the inland parts; and the invaders, if their enterprife mifcarried, might more eafily retreat. Some convenience, however, whatever it was, their pofition on the fhore afforded; for uniformity of practice

tice feldom continues long without good reafon.

A caftle in the Iflands is only a fingle tower of three or four ftories, of which the walls are fometimes eight or nine feet thick, with narrow windows, and clofe winding ftairs of ftone. The top rifes in a cone, or pyramid of ftone, encompaffed by battlements. The intermediate floors are fometimes frames of timber, as in common houfes, and fometimes arches of ftone, or alternately ftone and timber; fo that there was very little danger from fire. In the centre of every floor, from top to bottom, is the chief room, of no great extent, round which there are narrow cavities, or receffes, formed by fmall vacuities, or by a double wall. I know not whether there be ever more than one fire-place. They had not capacity to contain many people, or much provifion; but their enemies could feldom ftay to blockade them;

for

for if they failed in the firſt attack, their next care was to eſcape.

The walls were always too ſtrong to be ſhaken by ſuch deſultory hoſtilities; the windows were too narrow to be entered, and the battlements too high to be ſcaled. The only danger was at the gates, over which the wall was built with a ſquare cavity, not unlike a chimney, continued to the top. Through this hollow the defendants let fall ſtones upon thoſe who attempted to break the gate, and poured down water, perhaps ſcalding water, if the attack was made with fire. The caſtle of *Lochbuy* was ſecured by double doors, of which the outer was an iron grate.

In every caſtle is a well and a dungeon. The uſe of the well is evident. The dungeon is a deep ſubterraneous cavity, walled on the ſides, and arched on the top, into which the deſcent is through a narrow door,

by

by a ladder or a rope, fo that it feems impoffible to efcape, when the rope or ladder is drawn up. The dungeon was, I fuppofe, in war, a prifon for fuch captives as were treated with feverity, and, in peace, for fuch delinquents as had committed crimes within the Laird's jurifdiction; for the manfions of many Lairds were, till the late privation of their privileges, the halls of juftice to their own tenants.

As thefe fortifications were the productions of mere neceffity, they are built only for fafety, with little regard to convenience, and with none to elegance or pleafure. It was fufficient for a Laird of the *Hebrides*, if he had a ftrong houfe, in which he could hide his wife and children from the next Clan. That they are not large nor fplendid, is no wonder. It is not eafy to find how they are raifed, fuch as they are, by men who had no money, in countries where the labourers and artificers could fcarcely be fed.

The

The buildings in different parts of the Islands shew their degrees of wealth and power. I believe that for all the castles which I have seen beyond the *Tweed*, the ruins yet remaining of some one of these which the *English* built in *Wales*, would supply materials.

These castles afford another evidence that the fictions of romantic chivalry had for their basis the real manners of the feudal times, when every Lord of a seignory lived in his hold lawless and unaccountable, with all the licentiousness and insolence of uncontested superiority and unprincipled power. The traveller, whoever he might be, coming to the fortified habitation of a Chieftain, would, probably, have been interrogated from the battlements, admitted with caution at the gate, introduced to a petty Monarch, fierce with habitual hostility, and vigilant with ignorant suspicion; who, according to his general temper, or accidental

accidental humour, would have seated a stranger as his guest at the table, or as a spy confined him in the dungeon.

Lochbuy means the *Yellow Lake*, which is the name given to an inlet of the sea, upon which the castle of Mr. *Maclean* stands. The reason of the appellation we did not learn.

We were now to leave the *Hebrides*, where we had spent some weeks with sufficient amusement, and where we had amplified our thoughts with new scenes of nature, and new modes of life. More time would have given us a more distinct view, but it was necessary that Mr. *Boswell* should return before the courts of justice were opened; and it was not proper to live too long upon hospitality, however liberally imparted.

Of these islands it must be confessed, that they have not many allurements, but to

the

the mere lover of naked nature. The inhabitants are thin, provisions are scarce, and desolation and penury give little pleasure.

The people collectively considered are not few, though their numbers are small in proportion to the space which they occupy. *Mull* is said to contain six thousand, and *Sky* fifteen thousand. Of the computation respecting *Mull*, I can give no account; but when I doubted the truth of the numbers attributed to *Sky*, one of the Ministers exhibited such facts as conquered my incredulity.

Of the proportion, which the product of any region bears to the people, an estimate is commonly made according to the pecuniary price of the necessaries of life; a principle of judgment which is never certain, because it supposes what is far from truth, that the value of money is always the

the fame, and fo meafures an unknown quantity by an uncertain ftandard. It is competent enough when the markets of the fame country, at different times, and thofe times not too diftant, are to be compared; but of very little ufe for the purpofe of making one nation acquainted with the ftate of another. Provifions, though plentiful, are fold in places of great pecuniary opulence for nominal prices, to which, however fcarce, where gold and filver are yet fcarcer, they can never be raifed.

In the *Weftern Iflands* there is fo little internal commerce, that hardly any thing has a known or fettled rate. The price of things brought in, or carried out, is to be confidered as that of a foreign market; and even this there is fome difficulty in difcovering, becaufe their denominations of quantity are different from ours; and when there is ignorance on both fides, no appeal can be made to a common meafure.

This,

This, however, is not the only impediment. The *Scots*, with a vigilance of jealoufy which never goes to fleep, always fufpect that an *Englifhman* defpifes them for their poverty, and to convince him that they are not lefs rich than their neighbours, are fure to tell him a price higher than the true. When *Lefley*, two hundred years ago, related fo punctilioufly, that a hundred hen eggs, new laid, were fold in the Iflands for a penny, he fuppofed that no inference could poffibly follow, but that eggs were in great abundance. Pofterity has fince grown wifer; and having learned, that nominal and real value may differ, they now tell no fuch ftories, left the foreigner fhould happen to collect, not that eggs are many, but that pence are few.

Money and wealth have by the ufe of commercial language been fo long confounded, that they are commonly fuppofed to be the fame; and this prejudice has
fpread

spread so widely in *Scotland*, that I know not whether I found man or woman, whom I interrogated concerning payments of money, that could surmount the illiberal desire of deceiving me, by representing every thing as dearer than it is.

From *Lochbuy* we rode a very few miles to the side of *Mull*, which faces *Scotland*, where, having taken leave of our kind protector, Sir *Allan*, we embarked in a boat, in which the seat provided for our accommodation was a heap of rough brushwood; and on the twenty-second of *October* reposed at a tolerable inn on the main land.

On the next day we began our journey southwards. The weather was tempestuous. For half the day the ground was rough, and our horses were still small. Had they required much restraint, we might have been reduced to difficulties; for I think we had amongst us but one bridle.

We fed the poor animals liberally, and they performed their journey well. In the latter part of the day, we came to a firm and smooth road, made by the soldiers, on which we travelled with great security, busied with contemplating the scene about us. The night came on while we had yet a great part of the way to go, though not so dark but that we could discern the cataracts which poured down the hills on one side, and fell into one general channel that ran with great violence on the other. The wind was loud, the rain was heavy, and the whistling of the blast, the fall of the shower, the rush of the cataracts, and the roar of the torrent, made a nobler chorus of the rough music of nature, than it had ever been my chance to hear before. The streams, which ran cross the way from the hills to the main current, were so frequent, that after a while I began to count them; and, in ten miles, reckoned fifty-five, probably missing some, and having let some pass before they forced themselves upon my notice. At last we came to *Inverary*, where we found an inn, not only commodious, but magnificent.

The difficulties of peregrination were now at an end. Mr. *Boswell* had the honour of being known to the Duke of *Argyle*, by whom we were very kindly entertained at his splendid seat, and supplied with conveniences for surveying his spacious park and rising forests.

After two days stay at *Inverary* we proceeded southward over *Glencoe*, a black and dreary region, now made easily passable by a military road, which rises from either end of the *glen*, by an acclivity not dangerously steep, but sufficiently laborious. In the middle, at the top of the hill, is a seat with this inscription, *Rest, and be thankful.* Stones were placed to mark the distances, which the inhabitants have taken away, resolved, they said, *to have no new miles.*

In this rainy season the hills streamed with waterfalls, which, crossing the way, formed currents on the other side, that ran in contrary directions as they fell to the north or south of the summit. Being, by the favour of the Duke, well mounted, I went up and down the hill with great convenience.

From *Glencoe* we passed through a pleasant country to the banks of *Loch Lomond*, and were received at the house of Sir *James Colquhoun*, who is owner of almost all the thirty islands of the Loch, which we went in a boat next morning to survey. The heaviness of the rain shortened our voyage, but we landed on one island planted with yew, and stocked with deer, and on another containing perhaps not more than half an acre, remarkable for the ruins

ruins of an old caſtle, on which the oſprey builds her annual neſt. Had *Loch Lomond* been in a happier climate, it would have been the boaſt of wealth and vanity to own one of the little ſpots which it incloſes, and to have employed upon it all the arts of embelliſhment. But as it is, the iſlets, which court the gazer at a diſtance, diſguſt him at his approach, when he finds, inſtead of ſoft lawns and ſhady thickets, nothing more than uncultivated ruggedneſs.

Where the Loch diſcharges itſelf into a river, called the *Leven*, we paſſed a night with Mr. *Smollet*, a relation of Doctor *Smollet*, to whoſe memory he has raiſed an obeliſk on the bank near the houſe in which he was born. The civility and reſpect which we found at every place, it is ungrateful to omit, and tedious to repeat. Here we were met by a poſt-chaiſe, that conveyed us to *Glaſgow*.

To describe a city so much frequented as *Glasgow*, is unnecessary. The prosperity of its commerce appears by the greatness of many private houses, and a general appearance of wealth. It is the only episcopal city whose cathedral was left standing in the rage of Reformation. It is now divided into many separate places of worship, which, taken all together, compose a great pile, that had been some centuries in building, but was never finished; for the change of religion intercepted its progress, before the cross isle was added, which seems essential to a *Gothick* cathedral.

The college has not had a sufficient share of the increasing magnificence of the place. The session was begun; for it commences on the tenth of *October*, and continues to the tenth of *June*; but the students appeared not numerous, being, I suppose, not yet returned from their several homes. The division of the academical year into one session, seffion, and one recefs, seems to me better accommodated to the prefent ftate of life, than that variegation of time by terms and vacations derived from diftant centuries, in which it was probably convenient, and ftill continued in the *Englifh* univerfities. So many folid months as the *Scotch* fcheme of education joins together, allow and encourage a plan for each part of the year; but with us, he that has fettled himfelf to ftudy in the college is foon tempted into the country, and he that has adjufted his life in the country, is fummoned back to his college.

Yet when I have allowed to the univerfities of *Scotland* a more rational diftribution of time, I have given them, fo far as my inquiries have informed me, all that they can claim. The ftudents, for the moft part, go thither boys, and depart before they are men; they carry with them little fundamental knowledge, and therefore the

fupersuperstructure cannot be lofty. The grammar-schools are not generally well supplied; for the character of a school-master being there less honourable than in *England*, is seldom accepted by men who are capable to adorn it, and where the school has been deficient, the college can effect little.

Men bred in the universities of *Scotland* cannot be expected to be often decorated with the splendours of ornamental erudition, but they obtain a mediocrity of knowledge, between learning and ignorance, not inadequate to the purposes of common life, which is, I believe, very widely diffused among them, and which countenanced in general by a national combination so invidious, that their friends cannot defend it, and actuated in particulars by a spirit of enterprise, so vigorous, that their enemies are constrained to praise it, enables them to find, or to make their way to employment, riches, and distinction.

From

From *Glasgow* we directed our course to *Auchinleck*, an estate devolved, through a long series of ancestors, to Mr. *Boswell's* father, the present possessor. In our way we found several places remarkable enough in themselves, but already described by those who viewed them at more leisure, or with much more skill; and stopped two days at Mr. *Campbell's*, a gentleman married to Mr. *Boswell's* sister.

Auchinleck, which signifies a *stony field*, seems not now to have any particular claim to its denomination. It is a district generally level, and sufficiently fertile, but like all the *Western* side of *Scotland*, incommoded by very frequent rain. It was, with the rest of the country, generally naked, till the present possessor finding, by the growth of some stately trees near his old castle, that the ground was favourable enough to timber, adorned it very diligently with annual plantations.

Lord

Lord *Auchinleck*, who is one of the
Judges of *Scotland*, and therefore not
wholly at leisure for domestick business, or
pleasure, has yet found time to make
improvements in his patrimony. He has
built a house of hewn stone, very stately
and durable, and has advanced the value
of his lands with great tenderness to his
tenants.

I was, however, less delighted with the
elegance of the modern mansion, than with
the sullen dignity of the old castle. I clambered with Mr. *Boswell* among the ruins,
which afford striking images of ancient
life. It is, like other castles, built upon
a point of rock, and was, I believe, anciently surrounded with a moat. There is
another rock near it, to which the drawbridge, when it was let down, is said to
have reached. Here, in the ages of tumult
and rapine, the Laird was surprised and
killed by the neighbouring Chief, who

perhaps

perhaps might have extinguifhed the family, had he not in a few days been feized and hanged, together with his fons, by *Douglas*, who came with his forces to the relief of *Auchinleck*.

At no great diftance from the houfe runs a pleafing brook, by a red rock, out of which has been hewn a very agreeable and commodious fummer-houfe, at lefs expence, as Lord *Anchinleck* told me, than would have been required to build a room of the fame dimenfions. The rock feems to have no more dampnefs than any other wall. Such opportunities of variety it is judicious not to neglect.

We now returned to *Edinburgh*, where I paffed fome days with men of learning, whofe names want no advancement from my commemoration, or with women of elegance, which perhaps difclaims a pedant's praife.

The

The converfation of the *Scots* grows every day lefs unpleafing to the *Englifh*; their peculiarities wear faft away; their dialect is likely to become in half a century provincial and ruftick, even to themfelves. The great, the learned, the ambitious, and the vain, all cultivate the *Englifh* phrafe, and the *Englifh* pronunciation, and in fplendid companies *Scotch* is not much heard, except now and then from an old Lady.

There is one fubject of philofophical curiofity to be found in *Eainburgh*, which no other city has to fhew; a college of the deaf and dumb, who are taught to fpeak, to read, to write, and to practife arithmetick, by a gentleman, whofe name is *Braidwood*. The number which attends him is, I think, about twelve, which he brings together into a little fchool, and inftructs according to their feveral degrees of proficiency.

I do

I do not mean to mention the inſtruction of the deaf as new. Having been firſt practiſed upon the ſon of a conſtable of *Spain*, it was afterwards cultivated with much emulation in *England*, by *Wallis* and *Holder*, and was lately profeſſed by Mr. *Baker*, who once flattered me with hopes of ſeeing his method publiſhed. How far any former teachers have ſucceeded, it is not eaſy to know; the improvement of Mr. *Braidwood*'s pupils is wonderful. They not only ſpeak, write, and underſtand what is written, but if he that ſpeaks looks towards them, and modifies his organs by diſtinct and full utterance, they know ſo well what is ſpoken, that it is an expreſſion ſcarcely figurative to ſay, they hear with the eye. That any have attained to the power mentioned by *Burnet*, of feeling ſounds, by laying a hand on the ſpeaker's mouth, I know not; but I have ſeen ſo much, that I can believe more; a ſingle word, or a ſhort ſentence, I think, may poſſibly be ſo diſtinguiſhed.

It

It will readily be supposed by those that consider this subject, that Mr. *Braidwood*'s scholars spell accurately. Orthography is vitiated among such as learn first to speak, and then to write, by imperfect notions of the relation between letters and vocal utterance; but to those students every character is of equal importance; for letters are to them not symbols of names, but of things; when they write they do not represent a sound, but delineate a form.

This school I visited, and found some of the scholars waiting for their master, whom they are said to receive at his entrance with smiling countenances and sparkling eyes, delighted with the hope of new ideas. One of the young Ladies had her slate before her, on which I wrote a question consisting of three figures, to be multiplied by two figures. She looked upon it, and quivering her fingers in a manner which I thought very pretty, but of which I know not whether

ther

ther it was art or play, multiplied the fum regularly in two lines, obferving the decimal place; but did not add the two lines together, probably difdaining fo eafy an operation. I pointed at the place where the fum total fhould ftand, and fhe noted it with fuch expedition as feemed to fhew that fhe had it only to write.

It was pleafing to fee one of the moft defperate of human calamities capable of fo much help: whatever enlarges hope, will exalt courage; after having feen the deaf taught arithmetick, who would be afraid to cultivate the *Hebrides?*

Such are the things which this journey has given me an opportunity of feeing, and fuch are the reflections which that fight has raifed. Having paffed my time almoft wholly in cities, I may have been furprifed by modes of life and appearances of nature, that are familiar to men of

wider

wider survey and more varied conversation. Novelty and ignorance must always be reciprocal, and I cannot but be conscious that my thoughts on national manners, are the thoughts of one who has seen but little.

THE END.

www.ingramcontent.com/pod-product-compliance
Lightning Source LLC
Chambersburg PA
CBHW032027220426
43664CB00006B/385